WAR IN
THE AIR
1914–45

WAR IN THE AIR 1914–45

WILLIAMSON MURRAY

General Editor: John Keegan

SMITHSONIAN BOOKS

An Imprint of HarperCollinsPublishers

To Sir Michael Howard
who in the dark days of the 1970s
kept military history alive.

Text © Williamson Murray, 1999
Design and layout copyright © Cassell
First published in hardcover in Great Britain 1999
UK paperback edition 2002
The picture credits on p. 240 constitute an extension to this copyright page.

HarperCollins books may be purchased for educational, business, or sales
promotional use. For information, please write: Special Markets Department,
HarperCollins Publishers, 10 East 53rd Street, New York, NY 10022.

Published 2005 in the United States of America by Smithsonian Books
In association with Cassell
Wellington House, 125 Strand
London WC2R 0BB

Library of Congress Cataloging-in-publication data has been applied for.
ISBN-10: 0-06-083856-6
ISBN-13: 978-0-06-083856-0

Manufactured in Spain, not at government expense.

Cartography: Arcadia Editions Ltd.
Designer: Richard Carr
Picture research: Elaine Willis
Printed and bound in Spain

Title Page: *A formation of US Navy Grumman TBF-1 Avengers, one of the most
successful carrier-based torpedo bombers of the Second World War.*
Overleaf: *By V J-Day, nearly 8,000 P-51D Mustangs had left US aircraft factories,
providing a major contribution to the defeat of the Axis forces in Europe and the Imperial
Japanese forces in Asia and the Pacific.*

05   06   07   08   09   IM   10   9   8   7   6   5   4   3   2   1

Acknowledgements

I would like to thank the Aeronautics Department at the Smithsonian Air and Space Museum whose generosity in nominating me to hold the Charles Lindbergh chair provided the time to write this book.

Williamson Murray

Contents

KEY TO MAPS

Military units–types

⊠ infantry

▬ armoured

⌒ airborne

☂ parachute

Military units–size

XXX corps

XX division

X brigade

III regiment

II battalion

Military unit colours

Allied

German

Military movements

→ ground attack

⇒ air attack

General military symbols

⊥ field gun

☂ paratroop drop

✈ airfield

Geographical symbols

urban area

——— road

▬▬ railway

river

seasonal river

canal

border

≍ bridge

Yellow

Sea

anghai

Hon

Nag

PACIFIC   EAN

Map list

Chronology

World War I

European armies begin development of military aircraft.

1910

Establishment of French Air Service.

1911

Italians use aircraft against Turks in Libya by dropping modified grenades; aircraft used for reconnaissance in Mexican revolution.

1913

Germans found Imperial Air Service.

1914

August	Britain has 113 military aircraft; France 138; Germany 384; Russia 45; Austria 36.
August	Zeppelins bomb Liège.
August	British and French reconnaissance aircraft pick up movement of Schlieffen Plan.
26 August	First recorded aerial combat.
2 September	French pilot Corporal Louis Breguet reports swing of German army past Paris before the battle of the Marne.
December	First use of radio from aircraft to control indirect artillery fire.

1915

January	British aircraft raid Germany.
March	Frenchman Roland Garros mounts a machine-gun on his aircraft.

April	Fokker develops first machine-guns synchronized with propeller movement.
31 May	First Zeppelin raid on London by German Naval Air Service.
August	Fokker Eindekkers begin to ravage Allied reconnaissance flights.
Fall	Formation of German air squadrons led by successful aces.

1916

January	German aces Immelmann and Boelcke awarded the Pour le Mérite for shooting down their eighth enemy aircraft.
Spring	French achieve air superiority over Verdun battlefield. Form élite fighter units, the Cigognes (storks) to match Germans.
June	Russian air reconnaissance plays crucial role in success of the Brusilov offensive.
Summer	Heavy air battles between British and German airmen for air superiority over the Somme battlefield. British used aircraft in a ground attack role for the first time.
2 September	First Zeppelin shot down over Britain.

1917

April	Disastrous defeat of the Nivelle offensive, partially caused by German air superiority.
'Bloody April'	Serious losses suffered by Royal Flying Corps during battle of Arras amounting to a third of British air crews.
April	Emergence of large gaggles of fighter aircraft in the contest for air superiority.
Spring	Emergence of close air support mission.
May	First Gotha bomber raid on Britain: ninety-five killed and 260 wounded at Folkestone. War is taken to the civilian for the first time.
13 June	Second Gotha raid on London hits Liverpool Street Station: 162 dead, 432 wounded.

Summer	Appearance of British SE-5, the Sopwith Camel and the Bristol fighter provide temporary Allied air superiority on the Western Front.
September	British outrage at Gotha raids prompts vastly improved anti-aircraft defences, forcing the Germans to attack by night.
November	British aircraft along with tanks play a major role in the success at Cambrai.

1918

March	Introduction of new German aircraft the Fokker D.VII gives Germany the technical edge in the air in the first days of the March offensive.
Spring	Forty Gotha bombers sent to attack London are scattered or destroyed, ending the Gotha raids on Britain.
April	Formation of the Royal Air Force under Gen. Sir Hugh Trenchard.
April	Richthofen, 'the Red Baron', shot down and killed.
May	Trenchard attempts strategic bombing, targeting Germany's industrial heartland, the Ruhr.
8 August	RAF aircraft supporting the tanks play a major role in the success of British offensive.

Interwar Period

1919

Treaty of Versailles prohibits German possession of military aircraft.

Early 1920s

Douhet expounds his theories of strategic bombing.

RAF fights for survival and develops its own conceptions of strategic bombing.

1922

Washington Treaty indirectly contributes to creation of carrier fleets.

1925

Court-martial of US General Billy Mitchell for criticizing national defence.

1933

30 January   Hitler comes to power in Germany: Goering named Air Minister and Luftwaffe secretly initiates dive-bomber programme.

1935

First experiments with radar in Britain.

March   Germans announce Luftwaffe's existence due to confusion of their blue uniforms with doormen in Berlin.

Fall   Italians use mustard gas dropped from aircraft against barefoot tribal levies in Abyssinia.

1936

Summer   Ju-52 transport aircraft play major role in Spanish Civil War by flying Franco's Spanish Foreign Legion from Morocco to mainland Spain. Luftwaffe use voice radios which revolutionize air-to-air tactics.

1937

Dowding assumes control of Fighter Command and works to improve air defences with radar and radio communications.

December   Chamberlain government refuses funding for RAF bomber programme.

1938

Spring	Spitfire enters service with RAF, and the Ju 87b Stuka is supplied to the Luftwaffe.
September	Munich surrender partially the result of fears over Luftwaffe's capabilities.
Fall	Fighter Command receives Hurricanes in large numbers.

World War II: Europe

1939

September	Close air support plays major role in German success in Poland.

1940

9 April	German paratroopers capture Oslo airport and open door to capture Norwegian capital.
10 May	German glider infantry capture Fort Eben Emael in Belgium and pave way for the invasion of Army Group B.
13 May	German close air support attacks on French positions around Sedan breaks French artillery and clears the way for crossing of River Meuse by XIX Panzer Corps.
July–Oct	Battle of Britain: the first all-air battle in history is the first serious defeat for the German war machine.
September	Luftwaffe continues the Blitz on London and other British cities.
October	Italian air force bombs Athens.
November	Swordfish biplanes launched from HMS *Illustrious* wipe out half the Italian battle fleet at Taranto.

1941

7 April	German bombing of Belgrade kills 17,000 Yugoslavs.
21 May	German paratroopers begin assault on Crete.
June	US Army Air Corps is renamed the US Army Air Force.
22 June	Operation Barbarossa, the German invasion of the Soviet Union, begins with massive assault on Soviet air fields, crippling 1,000 Russian planes.
11 December	Hitler declares war on the United States, bringing the mighty American aircraft industry into the European War.

1942

January	Luftwaffe close to collapse, having lost 36 per cent of fighter pilots and 56 per cent of bomber crews since Barbarossa began.
Late May	British Bomber Command carries out 1,000 bomber raids on targets in Germany. Front line strength of Bomber Command is about 420 aircraft, and the rate of loss about one in twenty.
June	Supported by heavy bombing, the German Army captures Sevastopol.
19 November	Soviets launch massive attacks on both flanks of German forces attacking Stalingrad and trap Germans in city. Thus, Sixth Army must depend on aerial bridge. Despite Goering's promises to the Führer, winter conditions and Soviet attrition block the Luftwaffe's attempts at resupply.

1943

April	Allies finally cover the air gap in the central Atlantic.
April	Allied air power cuts off German air bridge to Tunisia.
Spring	Battle of the Ruhr: British Bomber Command severely damages the Ruhr.
July	Germans fail to gain air superiority over the battleground at Kursk.

July	Operation Husky: supported by a vast aerial umbrella, Allies land on Sicily.
27 July	Battle of Hamburg: Bomber Command virtually destroys city of Hamburg, leaving 50,000 dead and 800,000 homeless.
17 August	US Eighth Air Force attacks Schweinfurt/ Regensburg – loses sixty bombers shot down.
8–14 October	Eighth Air Force loses sixty bombers on a single attack on Schweinfurt and 148 bombers over the course of a week.
Winter (1943/4)	Bomber Command destroys much of Berlin, but in turn suffers terrible losses.

1944

Late February	'Big Week': US bombing operations with extensive support from long-range escort fighters (P-51s) target the German aircraft industry and begin process of wearing down Luftwaffe.
1 April	Strategic bombing forces of US and Britain come under Eisenhower's command and begin efforts to destroy the French transportation network.
May	Luftwaffe fighter force goes into decline from which it never fully recovers.
12 May	Eighth Air Force begins attacks on German petroleum industry in the Reich.
6 June	Operation Overlord: massive use of air power to drop paratroopers, support invasion attack, and prevent German reinforcements from reaching Normandy.
August	Bomber Command's first daylight raids over Germany since the early months of the war. Special targets this month include the V-weapon sites.
17 September	Operation Market Garden, the plan to capture a series of bridges over rivers and canals in Holland, begins with airlift of three Allied airborne divisions.

| September | Western Allies begin transportation effort to shut down German railroad network. |

1945

| 13 February | A controversial and massive night attack on Dresden by 773 Lancaster bombers creates a firestorm that devastates the city. |
| 8 May | VE Day. Bomber Command lost over 50 per cent of its air crews during the course of the war. |

World War II: The Pacific

1937

| July | China incident begins major war between China and Japan; Japanese air crews gain combat experience. |

1939

| | Japanese Zero fighter first flown. In the early months of the Pacific war, it seemed invincible. |

1941

Mid 1941	Chennault's volunteer air force, the 'Flying Tigers' destroys nearly 300 Japanese aircraft from their base in Burma during a six-month period.
7 December	Japanese launch 423 carrier aircraft in an attack on Pearl Harbor that destroys much of the American battle fleet.
8 December	Japanese attack on Clark Field in the Philippines destroys 200 American aircraft on the ground, leaving just fifty-seven planes in operable condition.
10 December	Ninety Japanese fighters attack British ships off Malaya, sinking HMS *Repulse* and HMS *Prince of Wales*.

1942

Late January	US carriers raid Marshalls.
18 April	Col. James Doolittle leads B-25 bombers in attack on Tokyo and other Japanese cities from carrier USS *Hornet*.
7–8 May	Battle of Coral Sea: first naval battle in which the fleets never see each other, reconnaissance and attacks being carried out by carrier-launched aircraft.
4 June	Battle of Midway: US fleet sinks four Japanese carriers for the loss of one. Japanese lose many irreplaceable pilots.
August	US marines land on Guadalcanal to capture and complete the air strip soon named Henderson Field. The bitter struggle to hold it and thus dominate the Solomon Islands continues for five months.
October	US naval squadrons receive the powerfully effective F6F Hellcat fighter.

1943

2–4 March	Battle of Bismarck Sea: US land-based air power entirely destroys large Japanese convoy of troop ships off New Guinea.
November	US central Pacific drive begins at Tarawa Atoll in the Gilbert Islands: depends entirely on carrier-based air forces being able to defeat Japanese land-based air forces.

1944

Spring	The new 'super bomber', the B-29, enters the war after a long and expensive developmental programme.
11 June	Battle of Philippine Sea ('the Marianas Turkey Shoot') begins. US forces secure land bases from which to launch long-range bomber raids on the Japanese home islands.
October	Air power is crucial in the battle of Leyte Gulf, which also witnessed the first suicidal kamikaze attacks by Japanese pilots.

One of the last developments of the Zero was the A6M6c, codenamed Zeke, with an uprated Sakae 31 engine, self-sealing fuel tanks and extra armament. It entered service in late 1944. The Zero remained in production throughout the war, with more than 10,000 being built.

November	Kamikaze attacks damage four US carriers, two battleships, two destroyers and two light cruisers.

1945

January	B-29 Superfortress attacks on Japanese cities continue to be launched from China and Saipan.
February	US forces capture Iwo Jima, a strategically vital island within fighter range of Tokyo.
8–9 March	Gen. Lemay orders low altitude fire bombing of Tokyo which destroys the Japanese capital and kills 83,000.
7 April	US fleet off Okinawa subjected to assault by 700 Japanese aircraft, half of them kamikazes.
6 August	First atomic bomb dropped on Hiroshima by the B-29 *Enola Gay*, leaving 80,000 dead.
8 August	Second atomic bomb dropped on Nagasaki.
15 August	Japan surrenders.

War in the Air

Bombs exploding on the Focke-Wulf aircraft plant at Bremen in northern Germany which was the target for this Eighth Air Force B-17G Fortress now heading for home – a USAAF base in East Anglia.

Introduction

AS THE NINETEENTH CENTURY ended, the technological capability of heavier-than-air flight remained a dream. Yet within less than five decades of the opening of the bloodiest century in man's history, the aeroplane had established itself as a permanent and essential component of military operations. And the dropping of atomic bombs on Hiroshima and Nagasaki suggested that air power by itself might be sufficient to end the human race.

From his earliest days, man has dreamt of flight, of liberating himself from the confines of land and sea. At the same time, soldiers and sailors have often thought about what flight might mean for them. In the French Revolution balloon flight allowed a few a glimpse of the other side of the hill. By the 1920s others saw flight as offering apocalyptic capabilities to military organizations – capabilities that would allow armies to reach into an enemy's heartland and destroy his cities and industry. In most respects the twentieth century has lived up to those expectations. It has extended the reach and destructive capabilities of war. Yet while it has expanded military reach, it has not shortened conflict. Instead, it has made war more destructive, more terrifying, and in the end more damaging. Moreover, air war in the twentieth century has found itself intimately intertwined with technological development as well as industrial capacity.

Above all, war in the air has involved a war of machines against machines. Yet, it has also found itself tied to its romantic origins. The image of the First World War fighter pilot – of Ball, Richthofen, Immelmann, and Boelcke – has remained alive and vibrant at the end of the twentieth century. The swaggering fighter pilot, master of his machine, still forms much of the self-image of those who fly the descendants of Spads, Fokkers and Nieuports, as well as being the public's picture of the modern aviator, a picture that has proved surprisingly resistant to tarnish even with the terrible casualty bills of the Second

World War. Winston Churchill's glowing tribute to those who flew in Fighter Command – words among the most eloquent in the English language: 'Never in the field of human conflict was so much owed by so many to so few' – also contributed to the perpetuation of this myth.

In a scene from the British comedy review *Beyond the Fringe*, a young man attempts to enlist in 'the few', only to be told that there are 'far too many'. The authors of that skit were closer to the mark than they realized, because war in the air has ultimately rested on the numbers of victims rather than the numbers of victors. For every ace there have been at least five enemy victims in the air, as well as a whole host of those who have destroyed themselves in accidents resulting from bad weather, night-time conditions, or their own carelessness.

In the First World War in particular there was a dichotomy between the image of the industrial age's knights and the grim reality of those who plastered themselves and their machines over the landscape. One

First World War squadron historian described the remains of an aircraft that had flown straight into a mountain as being an indistinguishable mass of metal, wood, flesh and fabric. Without parachutes, in machines designed as much by guesswork as by engineering expertise, airmen died by the thousand. Their survival rates were as bad as anything the infantry units experienced, except perhaps in the bloodiest battles. Of 1,437 RAF pilots sent to France

Captain Albert Ball, British fighter ace, having shot down his forty-third enemy aircraft and survived a crash landing. He lost his life, aged 20 years, on 7 May 1917, a day after scoring his forty-seventh victory. Captain Ball was awarded a posthumous Victoria Cross on 3 June.

between July and December 1917, 18 per cent had been killed, 26 per cent injured or reported sick, 20 per cent were missing, and 25 per cent sent home for various reasons, including combat fatigue, by 1 November 1918. On that date only 11 per cent still remained in France. At least most of those who died died relatively quick, sudden deaths, with few cases of permanent maiming or disfigurement; by definition, falling out of the sky in a burning or crumpled machine inevitably resulted in termination of pilot, aircraft, and those unlucky enough to be on board.

The advantage airmen possessed was that, unlike the poor bloody infantrymen, they could return from confrontations with death to warm barracks, good meals and even clean sheets. In their messes rugby scrums, drunken brawls and idle chatter at times removed the omnipresence of death's icy fingers. As a First World War squadron commander remarked about his Australian and Canadian pilots: 'Wonderful chaps, breath of the wide open spaces; great pilots, likely to destroy a mess or anything else in five minutes at a guest night.'

The casualty rates were even more appalling in the next conflict. At the height of the Battle of Britain, Fighter Command's squadrons were losing nearly a quarter of their pilots each month: dead, maimed or missing. A young German coming of age in 1941 had a better chance of surviving the war by joining the Waffen SS and fighting on the Eastern Front than by joining the Luftwaffe and flying a fighter in the great air battles of 1943 and 1944. Similarly, a young American had a better chance of surviving the war by joining the US Marine Corps and fighting on the islands of the Pacific, than he had in flying B-17s over Germany in 1943 and early 1944.

The statistics for Bomber Command underline this. Survival rates for Bomber Command aircrews suggest typical casualty rates for those who flew in both world wars. Out of every 100 flying personnel in active units in the command, 51 were killed on operations, 9 died in crashes in Britain, 3 were seriously injured in crashes, 12 were captured by the Germans (some injured), 1 was shot down but evaded capture, and only 24 survived the war untouched. Significantly, these figures include the relatively large number of crews who flew on active operations in the last half of 1944 and first half of 1945, when the command suffered relatively few casualties.

For most aircrews life was a grim attempt to escape the odds. A few made a difference. In the world of combat pilots they had the reflexes, instincts and natural self-discipline to thrive; if they survived the first several missions, they might go on to become great fighter or bomber pilots. There was a certain moment when they and their aircraft became one – where they in effect became 'natural born killers'. In the First World War only 4 per cent of French fighter pilots eventually became aces as a result of aerial combat; however, they shot down 50 per cent of the German aircraft officially accredited to French fighter pilots. Hans Rudel, the great Nazi dive-bomber pilot, was a mediocre pilot who barely made it through flight training; but at a certain moment his flying

Too close for comfort: a captured RAF Spitfire, seen from a Luftwaffe Heinkel He III bomber in a photograph released by Goebbels' Ministry of Propaganda during the Battle of Britain, summer 1940.

skills turned from mediocrity to complete mastery. A few could follow in the wake of the naturals and pick off the leavings. Most, however, like Patroclus, could dress in Achilles' armour, but were no more than fodder, content, in the words of Kiffin Rockwell of the Lafayette Escadrille, to 'fly along, blissfully ignorant, hoping for the best'.

Initially, war in the air involved extraordinarily close contact with death. The French ace Albert Deullin, who admittedly had a penchant for killing at close range, returned from a mission in early 1917 with his aircraft and flying suit drenched in the blood of a German pilot and observer he had executed at point-blank range. He remarked to his appalled crew chief, 'It is nothing. I shot from very close'.

While much of air power's mystique has centred on the romantic figure of the fighter pilot, it was those who flew bombers who fulfilled the mission that carried the hopes and dreams of theorists and prophets. Yet, for much of the period from 1914 to 1945 air power's potential, as represented by bombs on targets, remained potential rather than actual. As Clausewitz had warned at the end of the Napoleonic wars, 'everything in war is simple, but the simplest thing is difficult. The difficulties accumulate and end in producing a kind of friction that is inconceivable unless one has experienced war ... Countless minor incidents – the kind you can never foresee – combine to lower the general level of performance, so that one always falls short of the intended goal.' In fact, the same conditions – friction, ambiguity and uncertainty – govern war in the air that govern war on land or at sea. Bad weather, faulty intelligence, wind, night, faulty machines, inadequate technology and the recuperative ability of human organizations, all made the effects of bombing far less than predicted. Airmen might have learned much had they read Clausewitz, but such was their technological determinism that the past, its historians and its lessons had little relevance for their world or culture.

One of the difficulties of examining war in the third dimension is the fact that it presents historians and analysts with intractable problems in weaving together a coherent picture of operations, or even grasping the effects of such operations. The history of ground and naval operations in the twentieth century is easier to evaluate. With its ebb and flow, ground war provides patterns from which to construct narratives. The key events announce themselves, victors and vanquished are usually obvious, and one can trace outcomes to specific events that have given rise to climatic or crucial moments on the battlefield. Similarly, naval operations and the clash of fleets also seem to have a degree of clarity.

Air operations, however, possess little clarity. The inherent chaos, speed and lack of landmarks make it difficult to reconstruct even the pattern of events. The greatest problem, however, is that the effects of air operations are most often indirect. How, for example, does one calculate air power's impact on the enemy's capacity to conduct or even to manage his economy? Here one deals entirely in intangibles, even when the war is over: what options might the enemy have exercised either militarily or economically had he not been under air attack? Did air attacks lower his civilian or military morale and, if so, what impact did a decline in morale have on his ability to fight or produce? What levels of production could enemy industry have reached but for the damage occasioned by air attacks? Such questions still pose intractable problems for historians half a century later.

It is the effects of air war that are particularly difficult to evaluate, even after the documents have been declassified or uncovered by historians. It was even more difficult for those engaged in conducting air war to judge the military utility of their actions and efforts. In describing the air operations of the US Eighth Air Force against Nazi Germany in 1942 and 1943, the authors of the official history, *The Army Air Forces in World War II*, have captured the atmosphere and uncertainties that characterized air war from 1914 through to the Gulf War:

> The heavy bomber offensive was an impersonal sort of war and monotonous in its own peculiar way. Day after day, as weather and equipment permitted, B-17s and B-24s went out, dropped their load, and turned homeward. The immediate results of their

strikes could be photographed and assessed by intelligence officers in categories reminiscent of high school 'grades' – bombing was excellent, good, fair, or poor. But rarely was a single mission or series of missions decisive, whatever earlier theory had taught of sudden paralysis of a nation by strategic bombardment . . . The effects of bombing were gradual, cumulative, and during the course of the campaign rarely measurable with any degree of assurance . . . Drama hovered close to each plane which sortied . . . but as drama the big show itself was in 1942–1943 flat, repetitive, without climax. The bomber crew found its sense of accomplishment in the twenty-fifth mission, which, in theory, would bring rotation and relief, not in an island won, an enemy army's surrender.

That passage encompasses the nature of air war past, present, and probably future.

For those who read of the air war or saw planes from the ground there remained a romantic element. But for those who flew on operations in the years 1914–18 or 1939–45 there was little romance in their lives. War in the air was a grim struggle to maintain psychological equilibrium as those around were dying and to survive appalling odds. Gavin Ewart's poem, 'When a Beau Goes In' (referring to a Second

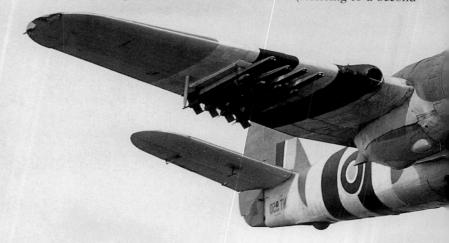

World War Beaufighter used by Coastal Command) captures that dark struggle in a way that no work of history can possibly do; it stands as a harsh reminder of what war really represented to those who flew in two all-consuming world wars.

When a Beau goes in,
Into the drink,
It makes you think,
Because, you see, they always sink
But nobody says 'Poor lad'
Or goes about looking sad
Because, you see, it's war,
It's the unalterable law,

Although it's perfectly certain
The pilot's gone for a Burton
And the observer too
It's nothing to do with you

And if they both should go
To a land where falls no rain
   nor hail
nor driven snow –
Here, there, or anywhere,
Do you suppose they care?

You shouldn't cry
Or say a prayer or sigh.
In the cold sea, in the dark
It isn't a lark
But it isn't original sin –
It's just a Beau going in.

An RAF Coastal Command Bristol Beaufighter Mk X anti-shipping strike fighter in June 1944, armed with eight 60-pound rocket projectiles and wearing D-Day invasion stripes.

CHAPTER ONE

The First World War

Machine-gunner of an O-1 two-seat reconnaissance fighter, a US-built Bristol F. 2B, dressed in leather helmet, great coat and gloves to combat the chills of altitude.

The First World War

I N AUGUST 1914 the long expected storm broke over the European
continent. Once again, as so often before, armies trampled across
the European landscape. This time, however, heavier-than-air machines
accompanied the troops. High above the soldiers, these early flying
machines made their solitary way back and forth to track the
movement of the great snake-like columns. Sometimes the generals
believed the reports of the pilots; often they refused to accept reports
which indicated that their opponents were doing the unexpected, and
thereby exploding their previous assumptions.

But at the crucial point in the German advance to the Marne, French
pilots based near Paris confirmed intelligence that the enemy was
swinging past the capital to the east. On 2 September 1914 Corporal
Louis Breguet reported field-grey columns were marching from west to
east – away from Paris toward the valley of the Ourcq, a report that
further flights confirmed. General Joseph-Simon Galliéni, commander

*One of the first British aircraft to be deployed to France in 1914 was the BE-2c
reconnaissance biplane, seen here in early national markings comprising Union Jack
and roundel on its fin. To war in wood and fabric!*

of Paris and the Sixth Army, who had strongly supported aviation before the war, utilized the intelligence to set in motion what eventually resulted in the battle of the Marne.

Aircraft proved equally useful on the Eastern Front, this time to the other side. German reconnaissance aircraft played a crucial role in locating and tracking the movement of the Russian forces that Hindenburg's Eighth Army encircled and destroyed at Tannenberg. But aircraft did more than reconnaissance; as German armies attacked Liège, Zeppelins from Cologne arrived overhead to bomb the Belgians. The Allies were revenged in October, however, when British naval aviators attacked the Zeppelin base in Düsseldorf and destroyed Zeppelin Z-9 in its shed.

All things considered, aircraft made a surprising impact on the events of 1914. This represented a quite remarkable achievement. Not until 1910 had heavier-than-air machines possessed capabilities that could have aided military organizations. Nevertheless, for the most part European armies and navies grasped those capabilities with enthusiasm. The prevailing views among generals and their staffs as well as the politicians was that the coming war would be short and mobile. Thus, the contestants threw their entire air forces into the contest and left little in reserve for reconstitution and expansion.

THE WAR IN THE WEST: 1915–16

But the war was not short, nor, at least in the west, was it a war of movement. After the failure of the Schlieffen Plan on the Marne, the opposing sides attempted to outflank their opponents in the race to the sea. That effort culminated in the British Expeditionary Force's courageous stand in Flanders, which finally brought the German advance to a halt. The battle of Langemark killed or maimed a whole corps of German university students, but it destroyed the professional British army as well. In both the east and west the opposing armies fought themselves out with casualty bills that numbered in the hundreds of thousands. The survivors dug in where the battle lines came to rest, and a great siege of the central powers – Germany and Austria–Hungary – began. The survivors in the small air services struggled to maintain their machines under winter conditions far from home bases – in late December 1914 a severe storm destroyed half the fragile aircraft of the Royal Flying Corps No. 6 Squadron, on its flying field in France.

THE FIRST BRITISH RAID ON GERMANY

From the very first days of the First World War, German Zeppelins were dropping bombs on Allied cities and in September 1914 British air units mounted the first raids on German soil to attack Zeppelin bases. On 25 September four Royal Naval Air Service (RNAS) Tabloids took off from seaplane carriers in the North Sea but, hampered by fog and inaccurate maps, the raid failed. However, on 8 October, an RNAS Tabloid succeeded in destroying a Zeppelin shed at Dusseldorf.

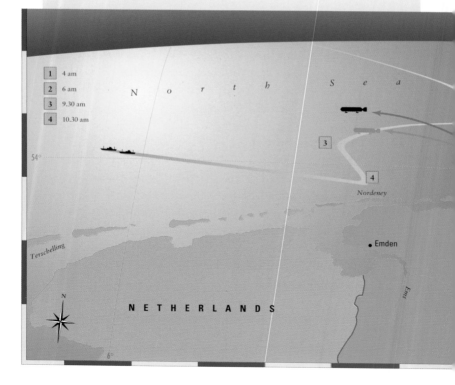

The initial problem confronting the Allies on the Western Front was twofold. On one hand the Germans held an important advantage in the firepower that modern rifles and machine-guns provided, because they would largely be on the defensive for the next three years. Extensive use of barbed wire strung in front of the trenches reinforced that advantage. On the other hand, while the gunners already understood the principles of indirect artillery fire before the war, they did not understand the full complexity of the factors that affected artillery accuracy until 1917: the effects of weather, humidity, and the wear of numerous shells on the gun barrel.

The first order of business for the Allies in the artillery war had to do with a more mundane issue, the making of accurate maps, since the French had not surveyed their own territory since the demise of the First Empire. The surveying of territory on the Allied side represented little

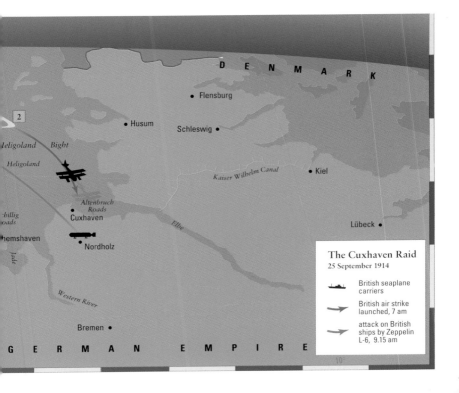

The Cuxhaven Raid
25 September 1914

British seaplane carriers

British air strike launched, 7 am

attack on British ships by Zeppelin L-6, 9.15 am

problem, but surveying German territory depended on matching up surveys with aerial photographs. Equally important for accurate artillery fire were aerial photographs of enemy defensive positions. Finally, aerial reconnaissance and observation of the enemy were crucial for operational intelligence. Thus, from the winter of 1914–15 reconnaissance achieved an undreamed-of importance. The armies of major powers scrambled not only to restore, but to expand flying schools supporting the infrastructure and the productive base of their air services.

As the nascent air forces struggled with the technical problems of aerial reconnaissance and the design and manufacturing problems of massive expansion in 1915, it became obvious that enemy aircraft represented an essential part of the equation. How to attack enemy reconnaissance aircraft while protecting one's own became the central focus of air operations for the rest of the First World War. Not surprisingly, some soon saw the aeroplane as more than a platform for observation, reconnaissance, and attacks on enemy reconnaissance aircraft. Perhaps the air services could use aircraft to attack enemy communications and supply lines – and possibly even to strike at his homeland.

In 1915, the first objective dominated aircraft employment. Aeroplanes began the business of artillery spotting. As early as December 1914 British aircraft had directed artillery fire from aircraft; and some British aircraft already possessed radio telegraphy. By the battle of Loos in September 1915 British fliers had worked out a clock code for calling the artillery shot in on targets. Nevertheless, at best, aircraft could only help in exchanges between a few artillery batteries. Their main purpose was the provision of aerial photographs on which divisional and corps staffs could plan their operations. The main burden of artillery spotting through much of the war was carried by the balloons. Tethered to the ground and flying at over 3,000 feet, balloons provided an outstanding survey of the surrounding landscape. Direct telephone contact with artillery batteries provided the means for controlling indirect artillery fire on enemy positions and batteries which were out of sight of ground observers.

The hydrogen-filled balloon had a crew basket hanging directly beneath it from which artillery spotters did their work. By their nature balloons were so dangerous that crews were provided with parachutes and given orders to jump as soon as enemy aircraft appeared. By spring 1916 French aircraft were carrying rockets to attack German balloons, which made their survival much less likely; incendiary bullets soon superseded rockets. On the other hand, as balloons were so essential to the artillery, ground troops set up strong anti-aircraft positions around operating balloons. The relatively low altitudes at which balloons worked and the strong anti-aircraft defences soon made them dangerous targets for enemy fighters.

By the end of 1914 air attacks on enemy reconnaissance aircraft had already begun. The first victims in the battle for control of the air occurred in the fleeting encounters between aircraft in 1914. Crews equipped with rifles and pistols took pot-shots at each other, any successes resulting more from luck than from skill. In spring 1915 the opponents were still struggling to come up with better methods of attacking enemy aircraft. Captain L. A. Strange of the Royal Flying Corps took off on 10 May 1915 carrying 150 feet of cable to which he had attached a lead weight, in the hope of entangling the cable in a German aircraft's propeller. He was also carrying a machine-gun. At 8,000 feet he spotted a German aircraft making for Menin and, concluding the cable was useless, he attacked with his machine-gun. While trying to change his ammunition drum, the Martinsyde flipped over. With no seat-belt, Strange dangled upside down, holding on for dear life to the strut and ammunition drum, which was supposed to have a quick release. As the upside-down Martinsyde headed down in a flat spin, Strange pulled himself back into the cockpit and regained control at 2,500 feet. What the Germans thought of the incident is not known.

The key to successful air-to-air combat was first discovered by the French and then refined by the Germans. In late 1914 Roland Garros, one of the leading pre-war French airmen, began work on a synchronizing gear to prevent the machine-gun from firing when the propeller blades passed in front of it; because the synchronizing gear did not work all the time, he shielded the propeller with deflector blades. Garros shot down three German aircraft in an eighteen-day period from 1 April 1915; but on 18 April he himself was shot down by anti-aircraft fire, and both he and his aircraft fell into German hands. As was so often the case in the First World War, the Germans took a first-class French idea and refined it. They were already working on such a device, but now they were spurred on by the knowledge that the French were also working on the problem. A Dutch entrepreneur in Germany, Anthony Fokker, and his design team evolved a successful interrupter gear that prevented the machine-gun from firing when the propeller was directly in front of it. Offered the chance to test the mechanism, Fokker declined at the last moment and left it to German pilots to test the new technology.

Beginning in August 1915 the Germans, flying the Fokker Eindekker, took an increasing toll of British and French aircraft in the west. Because the Germans were on the defensive in that theatre, the Eindekkers remained over German-held territory and none fell into Allied hands. Allied pilots attempted various makeshift devices to get

Drawing of the Fokker Eindekker E.III, the first true fighter. Fitted with the Fokker interrupter gear, the Eindekker became the mount for the first German aces including Oswald Boelcke and Max Immelmann in 1915.

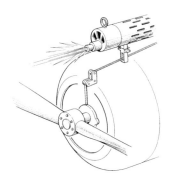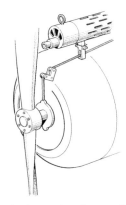

The interrupter gear on a machine-gun prevented it firing when the propeller was passing in front of it. Inspired by the capture of a Morane aircraft belonging to French ace Roland Garros, who had installed a forward-firing machine-gun firing through a propeller fitted with brass deflector plates, Dutch designer Anthony Fokker developed a simple engine-driven system of cams and push-rods which operated the trigger of a Parabellum machine-gun once during each revolution of the propeller. It was first fitted to the German Fokker E.1 in 1915.

round the propeller problem. Captain Lanoe Hawker strapped a machine-gun on the side of his Scout with a slightly downward trajectory in order to miss the propeller. In late July 1915 he actually shot down a German reconnaissance aircraft flying straight and level, for which action he received a Victoria Cross – deserved more for his flying skill than for his bravery.

With their technical advantage a small group of Fokker pilots began shooting down increasing numbers of Allied aircraft. Led by two superb pilots, Max Immelmann, 'the Eagle of Lille', and Oswald Boelcke, who flew together, the Germans developed embryonic air-to-air tactics. Gaining height advantage over their opponents, the Germans attacked out of the sun, so that more often than not their opponents never saw them. Thus came the British aphorism that stood the test of time in two world wars: 'Beware the Hun in the sun.' So successful were the Fokkers that Sir Hugh Trenchard, commander of the Royal Flying Corps in France, ordered that at least three fighting machines must cover reconnaissance missions.

Max Immelmann, known as 'The Eagle of Lille', was one of the fathers of fighter tactics. He was shot down by an RFC FE. 2b in June 1916, having scored fifteen victories.

The French enjoyed considerable success over their lines throughout the summer of 1915; but the appearance of the Fokkers in late summer impacted even more decisively on their operations than on those of the British. The French stayed too long with the aircraft types that had given them superiority in the spring of 1915. Thus, the devastating impact of the Fokkers severely affected French operations over the whole front. It also forced the French to move from daylight bombing operations to night-time operations, with all the difficulties in navigation and target location that such operations entailed.

Immelmann and Boelcke were the first real heroes of the air war. Each received the Pour le Mérite awards, the 'Blue Max', in mid January 1916 for shooting down their eighth enemy aircraft. Their fame had much to do with the grim struggle on the ground, which seemed to have too much heroism in its slaughter, but no identifiable heroes. Yet the German tactical approach remained largely defensive. They flew small patrols over their own territory; moreover, the German high command parcelled the Fokkers out among the various reconnaissance and balloon squadrons. Thus, while the Germans inflicted increasingly heavy casualties on their opponents, they failed to obtain anything resembling air superiority.

Throughout 1915 the Germans remained on the defensive and used their army reserves against Russia and in the Balkans. For their part, the Allies launched a series of offensives that resulted in heavy casualties, particularly among French forces. Incremental improvements in artillery tactics, which depended on the connection between aerial observation and reconnaissance, were not sufficient to break the deadlock on the Western Front. On the other side of the no-man's-land, the Germans were constructing increasingly sophisticated defences with deep dugouts, massive belts of barbed wire and additional trench lines to which defenders could fall back. In fact, both sides were adapting and innovating under the pressures of war, on the ground and in the air. In biological terms the Western Front was a complex adaptive process out of which modern war would eventually emerge – but the cost would be enormous.

The British exacerbated their problems in the air by a casual approach to training that sent pilots overseas with as little as five hours solo flying time, and treated the training of observers in the most casual fashion. The future air marshal Sholto Douglas described this training policy as 'sheer murder', which it was. Moreover, the difficulties of economic mobilization, for which none of the major powers had prepared, were affecting everything from the production of artillery shells to the production of aircraft.

In December 1915 the chief of the German General Staff and High Command, General Erich von Falkenhayn, determined to fight a battle of attrition against the French at Verdun. The German attack began in February with a massive artillery bombardment, followed by heavy infantry attacks. In the muddled thinking that so often passed for military competence in the First World War, Falkenhayn never intended to overwhelm the French defences. Rather he hoped to entice the French into feeding their reserves into a meat-grinder battle in which German artillery would wreck the French army. However, advancing down the right bank of the Meuse in the early attacks, the Germans came increasingly under heavy French artillery fire from the left bank. As Marshal Philippe Pétain summed it up: 'These people don't know their business.' The Germans failed equally in the air battle over Verdun. They set up barrier patrols which minimized the advantage they had possessed with the Fokkers at the beginning of the battle. But the French soon introduced a new aircraft, the Nieuport 11, the first aircraft exclusively designed for the fighter mission. Called '*le Bébé*' by its pilots, the Nieuport was superior in speed and manoeuvrability to the Fokker. As the French still lacked synchronized machine-guns, the Nieuport mounted its weapons on its upper wings – which made for difficulty in loading new drums of ammunition – but the aircraft's other characteristics gave the French considerable advantages over their opponents.

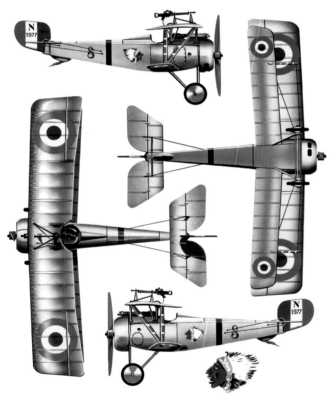

The French Nieuport 17 fighter was an outstandingly fast and agile aircraft. It is seen here in the colours for Lafayette Escadrille, *the American volunteer unit, known as* 'The Braves', *which joined the French Air Force in April 1916.*

By spring 1916 a combination of better aircraft and poor German tactics gave the French important advantages in the artillery battle. Moreover, the French now possessed rockets which enabled them to devastate German artillery balloons; on one day French pilots shot down five German balloons. By June the French had fought off the assault on Verdun, and while their ground forces had suffered fearfully, the Germans had lost almost as heavily – a casualty bill they could not afford, given the fact that they were fighting an international coalition.

Things went no better for the Germans elsewhere on the Western Front in 1916. After a heavy preparatory bombardment, British infantry went over the top at the Somme on 1 July 1916. The first day's attack was a disaster for the attacking forces, which suffered nearly 50 per cent casualties (over 57,000 men). The scale of that disaster, however, has obscured the heavy pressure British forces placed on German defenders for the remainder of the Somme battles, which finally burned out in late October. Falkenhayn demanded that German troops hold every square yard of their trenches and that, when a portion of the trench system was lost, German forces recover it immediately, regardless of its importance. Consequently, even more than elsewhere, the Germans packed their infantry into front-line trenches where the sheer weight of British artillery bombardments took a heavy toll on the defenders.

Two other factors exacerbated the German situation. First, the mobilization of the British economy now provided the British Expeditionary Force (BEF) with a mountain of shells to blast away at German defensive positions. An inelegant way to attack, certainly, but effective, particularly given the enemy's penchant for packing his front line trenches with infantry, all within easy range of British artillery. What the Germans termed 'the battle of *matériel*' had begun with a vengeance, a battle in the long run overwhelming to German tactical and operational excellence.

The second factor working against the Germans had to do with the air war over the Somme. That battle had turned as much against them as it had for them at Verdun. By early July 1916 the Royal Flying Corps

(RFC), with help from the French in Nieuport 11s, had redressed its inferiority vis-à-vis the Fokkers. With superior numbers, the British dominated the skies over the Somme – a crucial advantage in the artillery battle below. British reconnaissance and spotting aircraft flew mainly unimpeded by the Germans, while British fighters largely closed down German reconnaissance.

Yet the cost was high. In the first days of the Somme, the British lost 20 per cent of their flying strength. Cecil Lewis, who flew during this period and afterwards wrote one of the great works of literature about the war (*Sagittarius Rising*) indicates that pilots lasted barely three weeks during the heavy fighting. Hugh Dowding almost ended his career by requesting his squadron be relieved after having suffered 50 per cent casualties; he was sent home to command a training squadron and never brought back to the Western Front. Losses remained high throughout the battle, and Britain was still sending out pitifully trained replacements. The sacrifices that Trenchard imposed on his air units were undoubtedly called for because of the importance of the Royal Flying Corps to the ground battle; yet Trenchard made little contribution to improving the haphazard training programme at home – and this contributed directly to his high losses in France. By mid November the RFC had lost 308 pilots killed, wounded or missing, while a further 268 had been sent home – a total of 576 from a force that had begun the battle with 426 pilots.

Much of the blame had to do with the casual British approach towards training. In October 1916 the director of the RFC in Britain reported that 'short training was a consequence of the number of casualties and not the casualties of the shortness of training'. Such muddled thinking only hastened the enemy's recovery as a new generation of German aircraft came into service in late 1916. A year later this mindset led authorities in Britain to reject a proposal for aircrew parachutes not only because they were too heavy and difficult to operate, but also because they might diminish the fighting edge of those who flew. Unlike the air services of the other powers, the Royal

The DH 2 was the Royal Flying Corps' first single-seat fighter. Armed with one forward-firing .303 inch Lewis machine-gun, the compact pusher aircraft entered service in 1916 and was the mount for two RFC pilots who won the VC, Majors Lionel Rees and Lanoe Hawker.

Flying Corps refused to train non-commissioned officers to fly. When the supply of public schoolboys began to run out in 1917, the British turned to the Empire, especially Canada and Australia. There was, moreover, a desperate amateurism to the British effort that contrasted with the harsh professionalism of the Germans. Boelcke, a true romantic hero who had risked his life to save a young French boy from drowning, was already laying down a set of guidelines for air-to-air combat that are almost as relevant today as they were then. Fighter pilots, according to Boelcke, needed to gain the advantage before they engaged the enemy; height and having the sun behind one's back and in the enemy's eyes were crucial advantages. In air-to-air combat one needed to fire short bursts at close range, not splatter shots all over the sky. If attacked, a fighter pilot should turn into his attacker and attack head on. Finally, fighter aircraft should work together as a team.

There was in these years a wide dichotomy between the romantic reports in newspapers and the realities of air-to-air combat. Given how little firepower fighter aircraft possessed, combat took place at very close range. The historian John Morrow, Jr., tells how one French pilot, Albert Deullin, avenged the death of a close friend by blowing a Fokker out of the sky at a range of ten metres: 'The fellow was so riddled that vaporized blood sprayed on my hood, windshield, cap, and goggles.

Naturally, the descent from 2,600 metres was delicious to contemplate.'

Since few fliers carried parachutes until late in the war, many jumped to their deaths rather than burn up as their shot-up machine spiralled towards the earth. Whatever happened to those unlucky enough to be shot down or crash, the results were gruesome enough. As the British doggerel put it:

> The young aviator lay dying.
> As in the hangar he lay, he lay,
> To the mechanics who round him were standing
> These last parting words he did say:

> Take the cylinders out of my kidneys
> The connecting rod out of my brain,
> From the small of my back take the camshaft,
> And assemble the engine again.

THE AIR WAR IN OTHER THEATRES, 1914–16:

In the spring of 1915 the British attacked the Dardanelles in order to get at Constantinople and force Turkey out of the war. If the operation had succeeded, it would have reopened the main supply route to Russia, and this would have helped the hard-pressed tsarist armies substantially. But the fall of Constantinople might have had even greater indirect effects, for Bulgaria and Romania were undecided as to which side to join. A British success at Gallipoli might have persuaded them to join the Allied camp and the resulting threat to Austria–Hungary would have forced the Germans to shut down their offensive against Russia and turn their full attention to the Balkans.

But plagued by bad luck and poor leadership, the Gallipoli campaign was a dismal failure. As Winston Churchill commented, 'the terrible ifs accumulate'. Nevertheless, aircraft were active in it from the beginning. Commander Charles Samson of the Royal Navy established a small force of aircraft on the Greek island of Tenedos – but of thirty aircraft

RFC RE. 8 two-seat reconnaissance aircraft, known as the 'Harry Tate', from the Middle East Brigade in Palestine observing Turkish shipping over the Sea of Galilee.

boxed up and sent out from Britain in March 1915, only five were in flying condition when unpacked. With those aircraft Samson and his pilots photographed the main Turkish positions on the peninsula and gave General Sir Ian Hamilton and his staff considerable knowledge of the enemy's defences. Lacking machine-guns, Samson and his pilots attempted to harry the Turks by throwing iron spikes down on them. What the Turks thought of the spikes whistling down from above – and rarely hitting anything – is not known.

Samson's aircraft then supported British and Anzac (Australian and New Zealand) troops ashore by spotting for navy ships. With a one-way radio telegraph, they reported the fall of shells by radio to the ships; the Royal Navy's ships then used searchlights and Morse to reply. On 25 April the landings began. Samson had a ringside seat from his aircraft, but he could only watch as British soldiers attempted to rush the Turkish machine-guns from the decks of the landing ship, the *River Clyde*, and were shot down by the hundreds. From his vantage point Samson saw the blue sea turn red around the *River Clyde*, while the ripples of the sea were a ghastly pink. In 1915 aircraft could provide photographs; they could provide intelligence; and, as happened at Suvla Bay, they could report the hills clear of Turkish positions and troops. But they could not make up for commanders who lacked all initiative, competence and drive. The collapse of the August 1915 attack on Suvla Bay signalled the failure of the one strategic opportunity the Allies enjoyed to break the deadlock in the west.

Aircraft played a useful but less dominant role in other theatres. Part of the reason lay in the style of war that was occurring elsewhere. In the east the Austro-Hungarians and Russians were unable to establish air forces of the quality and quantity of those on the Western Front, while Anglo-French pressure forced the Germans to deploy their best air units

The first four-engine bomber to become operational during the First World War was the Russian Ilya Mouromets of the Czar's Squadron of Flying Ships. Built by the Russo-Baltic Wagon Factory and designed by Igor Sikorsky, who later built helicopters in the USA, the bombers could carry up to 1,500 pounds of bombs and a crew of sixteen!

in the west. In the Russian case, the difficulties confronting tsarist military forces on the ground and in the air reflected as much the incompetence of the regime and its administration (in military as well as in civilian spheres) as Russia's backwardness. By August 1914 Igor Sikorski, who was to have an extraordinary career in aviation in the United States after the war, had already designed and produced a great military aircraft, the four-engined Ilya Mouromets. The Ilya Mouromets possessed a range of 185–250 miles, but Russian military leaders preferred less capable single-engined aircraft that they could produce in larger numbers.

Because the Germans wrote the history of the Eastern Front, the battle of Tannenberg has received undue attention. While the Russians suffered a major defeat at that battle, their main attention focused on Austria–Hungary and in the late summer and autumn of 1914 they dealt the Austro-Hungarian armies serious defeats that almost knocked their Habsburg enemies out of the war. These battles on the Eastern Front continued well into winter and only significant German

help held the Russian steamroller short of the Hungarian plains. But the savage battle used up most of Russia's stocks of ammunition and equipment, including aircraft. Counting on a short war, the tsarist bureaucracy failed to mobilize Russia's resources and industrial potential until too late. Russian armies and air units were thus in dreadful shape when the Germans attacked at Gorlice/Tarnów in May 1915. Sikorski's Mouromets proved useful, but lack of foresight led to few being available.

In general aircraft proved less useful in the east, because the force-to-space ratio was so much lower than in the west. Consequently, it was easier to achieve breakthroughs and harder to stabilize the front once enemy forces were in the open. The German advance continued through the late summer and drove the Russians entirely out of Poland. German aircrews enjoyed air superiority, as much due to Russian failures as to the superiority of German aircraft and pilots. Given the capabilities of the aircraft, this superiority largely translated into an important advantage in terms of reconnaissance. The Russians remained largely blind to what their opponents were doing, while the Germans possessed a relatively clear picture of the movements of their opposition.

Despite the pleas of General Erich Ludendorff and Field Marshal Paul von Hindenburg for a massive invasion of Russia, Falkenhayn shut down the offensive in the east and transferred German forces to the west for the attack on Verdun. In the spring of 1916, without informing anyone in Berlin, his Austrian allies transferred most of their reserves to the Italian theatre for a major offensive. But by the summer of 1916 Russia's military forces had undergone an astonishing recovery. While the number of aircraft available were still minuscule compared to the numbers available in the west – over the entire Eastern Front the Russians had deployed only 250 aircraft in commission on 1 June 1916 – their capabilities had improved immensely. Careful photo reconnaissance of Austrian positions played a major role in the collapse of Austro-Hungarian armies before the Brusilov offensive in early June.

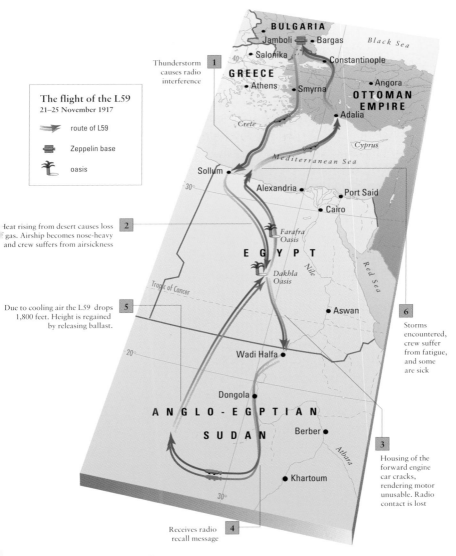

The flight of the L59
21–25 November 1917

route of L59

Zeppelin base

oasis

1 Thunderstorm causes radio interference

2 Heat rising from desert causes loss of gas. Airship becomes nose-heavy and crew suffers from airsickness

5 Due to cooling air the L59 drops 1,800 feet. Height is regained by releasing ballast.

6 Storms encountered, crew suffer from fatigue, and some are sick

3 Housing of the forward engine car cracks, rendering motor unusable. Radio contact is lost

4 Receives radio recall message

LONG DISTANCE ZEPPELIN RECORD

In November 1917 Lieutenant Commander Ludwig Bockholt was ordered to ferry 14 tons of supplies aboard his naval airship L 59 from Bulgaria to German East Africa, a distance of 3,600 miles. A few miles short of his destination Bockholt was ordered to turn back, and landed back in Bulgaria after a 95-hour flight that covered 4,200 miles.

That success in turn – the last tsarist armies would enjoy – forced Falkenhayn to abandon Verdun and rush reinforcements to the east. Continuing difficulties in the east throughout the summer exacerbated German difficulties on the Somme. But the Russians had shot their bolt. Grimly furious at the regime's incompetence, Russia was about to enter the dreadful era of revolution, civil war and Soviet rule.

The Austrians were not only involved on the Eastern Front, but also confronted the Italians along the Dolomite Alps. Aircraft proved as important there as on the Western Front. The Italians had entered the war in May 1915 when it appeared that the attack on Gallipoli would defeat the Turks and end the war in the near future. Instead, the Italians found themselves launching badly planned attacks against almost impregnable positions along the Alps. In the end these attacks and the war in general would cost them over 600,000 dead.

The Italians and Austrians proved less able to work out the complexities of infantry, artillery and aircraft co-operation that was emerging on the Western Front. Yet in 1915 the Italians were the only country with an aircraft (the Caproni Ca 1) whose sole purpose was bombing. Even before the war Giulio Douhet, the future prophet of air power, was arguing for its potential to destroy an enemy's morale. Still, what the Italians had in 1915 was insignificant: a few leaflet-dropping flights over Trieste failed to impress even the Austrians. By 1916, however, the Italians had substantially more Capronis and they launched a number of heavy strikes at the Austrian railroads supporting the Isonzo front. But the Austrians were also improving their fighter defences with help from their German allies. The result was that Italian bomber losses soon mounted, and the Italians were forced to move to night bombing, where the safety of darkness did little to improve accuracy.

THE INCONCLUSIVE BATTLES: 1917

In September 1916 the pendulum of the air war began to swing back towards the Germans. Boelcke returned to active duty on the Western Front in the desperate struggle on the Somme; he resumed his efforts to create a more coherent approach to air tactics by inculcating his precepts into the minds of those flying under his command. There were those like René Fonck who, because of their remarkable eyesight and reflexes, could kill at great distances. Fonck himself honed his natural abilities by potting away at coins tossed in the air. But Boelcke understood that most fighter pilots lacked such skills, and therefore needed closer ranges. As Fonck's colleague Alfred Heurtaux inelegantly put it, shooting down aircraft was like shooting 'a cow in a corridor'. By late 1916 air-to-air combat was no longer an affair of single pilots; it had turned into a contest of larger and larger groups of fighter aircraft working together. The French had started the trend at Verdun, but in September Boelcke and the Germans created *Jagdstaffeln* (fighter squadrons) whose business was to drive enemy fighters out of the sky so that they could not disturb German reconnaissance aircraft.

The Germans were considerably aided in their efforts by the introduction of the Albatros D.III. Superior to everything in the Allied inventory until the arrival of the Camel in mid 1917, the Albatros provided Boelcke and his pilots a better opportunity for executing the new tactics. The result was that the Royal Flying Corps suffered increasingly heavy losses as the Somme battle burned itself out. Still plagued by a weak training programme, the life expectancy of RFC aircrews had dropped to less than a month by November 1916. The Germans also suffered serious losses since they possessed so few Albatros planes. Boelcke himself was killed in a mid-air collision with another pilot at the end of October. The Germans held a great funeral for their fallen hero in Cambrai cathedral.

While Field Marshal Douglas Haig, commander of the British Expeditionary Force, sought the final decisive push on the Somme (not, in fact, to come for another two years), French troops under command of General Robert Nivelle attacked the German positions at Verdun and regained all the territory lost in that battle. Nivelle's success resulted from the introduction of innovative combined arms tactics, which the French had been working on over the past two years –

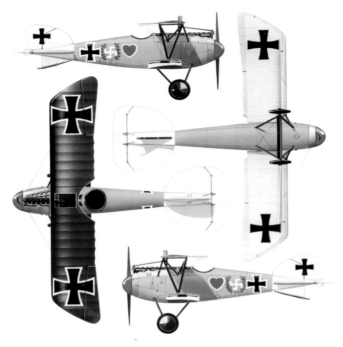

The German Albatros D.III fighter flown by German ace Werner Voss with Jasta 5 in 1917. When he was shot down and killed by an RFC SE-5a on 23 September 1917, Voss was credited with forty-eight victories making him the fourth highest scoring German pilot.

admittedly at heavy cost. Aircraft support with reconnaissance and artillery spotting had been an integral part of the evolution.

Shortly after Nivelle's success, Marshal Joffre finally fell from his position as French commander-in-chief. Pétain was his obvious replacement, but his dour and pessimistic nature failed to recommend him to politicians, who were desperate to find a solution to the disastrously costly conflict. So they selected Nivelle, and he responded by claiming that he had discovered the method that would achieve decisive success in spring 1917. In fact, Nivelle's offensive might well have achieved a major success except for three factors. The first was that the Germans had changed their entire defensive scheme. Over the autumn and winter of 1916–17 they created the tactics and doctrine for a defence in depth – a system that took the great bulk of their infantry and artillery out of range of enemy artillery. Strong points and machine-gun nests, manned by the best troops in the German army, would now break up and dislocate Allied attacks, while the bulk of German infantry awaited the best moment to counter-attack. The new system was deeper and more flexible, and represented a tactical system against which the French had no experience. The second factor lay in the German withdrawal from the positions they had held for the first two years of the war to better sited and prepared positions.

The third factor had to do with the situation in the air. In April 1917 German superiority with the Albatros reached its height at the moment when the Nivelle offensive along the Chemin des Dames began. Consequently, aided by an early warning system based on reports from the anti-aircraft units, German fighter squadrons received timely warnings of French air operations. Their response virtually shut down French reconnaissance and artillery observation flights; the Germans also inflicted substantial damage on French balloon units spotting for the artillery. Thus, French infantry went over the top with little intelligence on German defences, while the Germans were well informed on what the French were doing. While the loss of air superiority by itself was probably not decisive, it certainly exacerbated French difficulties along the Chemin des Dames. The failure of the Nivelle offensive, with heavy losses, came close to causing Allied defeat as mutinies broke out throughout the French army.

If April 1917 was a bad month for the French, it was a good month for the British army in its limited offensive in front of Arras. But the month was a disaster for the Royal Flying Corps – it was known as 'Bloody April' in recognition of the losses that enveloped British flying units. Trenchard's constantly aggressive policies, whether his air units had the advantage or not, resulted in such high losses that the training establishment in Britain never caught up with the demand. As a result, British fliers, as had been the case in 1916, were still arriving on the Western Front with substantially fewer training hours than their

German opponents; new pilots in May 1917 appear to have had less than twenty hours flying time – an improvement over 1916, but not much. One observer noted that many could not fly, much less fight. As a result the new arrivals had little chance to gain the experience required for survival in the killing arena of air-to-air combat.

Worse still, the British planes were distinctly inferior to the Albatros, which predominated in the German units opposite. Manfred von Richthofen commanded *Jagdstaffel* 11 on the Flanders front and was at

3 A small group of aircraft follow after initial attack to finish off isolated or damaged enemy aircraft

1 Attacking formation gains advantage of height, stalks the enemy formation using any possible advantage of cloud cover and then attacks, diving with the sun behind

the height of his skill as a fighter pilot. Over the course of the month, Richthofen shot down twenty-one British aircraft, including four on the 29th alone. Between 4 April and 8 April the Royal Flying Corps lost 75 planes in combat, with 19 aircrew killed, 13 wounded, and 73 missing. The situation did not improve over the course of the month. Flying obsolete aircraft, British pilots were committed to an operational approach that condemned them to seek out enemy aircraft aggressively, while the Germans could pick and choose where to fight. Those flying in particularly obsolete aircraft, such as the Sopwith 1½ Strutters

2 Unable to observe the approach of the enemy until the last moments before attack, even then defensive fire is made inaccurate, attempting to fire at aircraft flying 'out of the sun'

THE HUN IN THE SUN
By 1917, German fighters were hunting in packs known as 'Circuses', the most successful of which was von Richthofen's. In 'Bloody April', the Richthofen Flying Circus scored no less than eighty-three victories out of a total German bag of 150 British aircraft, mostly outdated reconnaissance machines.

Manfred von Richthofen, ace of aces. A former cavalry officer, Manfred Freiherr von Richthofen joined the Imperial German Air Service in May 1915 as an observer/air gunner. After training as a pilot, he scored his first victory, an RFC FE.2b, in September 1916. As his score rose steadily, he was given command of Jagdgeschwader Nr 1 which became known to the Allies as the 'Richthofen Flying Circus'. His personal aircraft were usually painted red, which led to him being dubbed 'The Red Baron' by British pilots. Having been awarded the 'Blue Max', von Richthofen became a national hero. His exploits filled German newspaper headlines. By the time he was shot down by Captain A. Roy Brown's Sopwith Camel on 21 April 1918 his score had risen to eighty victories.

and the Nieuports, were slaughtered. In his book *The Rise of the Fighter Aircraft, 1914–18*, Richard P. Hallion quotes one formation commander who exclaimed, after losing two aircraft out of his flight of six Strutters (the other four were all damaged): 'Some people say the Sopwith two-seaters are bloody fine machines, but I think they are more bloody than fine!'

In addition to these successes, the Germans were expanding their air operations to include a significant innovation: close air support. While both the British and French had launched a number of attacks against railroad stations, bivouacs, and other rear-area targets, no one had yet made major efforts to support the infantry across the killing zone with aircraft. In the Arras battle the Germans introduced bombers to support their infantry with machine-guns, grenades and bombs. At Messines in early June these aircraft held up a successful British advance that was rolling forward after the explosion of a massive mine had destroyed most of the main German defensive positions.

By now war in the air had moved from duels between single aircraft to large formations contesting air superiority over segments of the front in swirling combat. On 30 April the Germans put up two large groups of twenty aircraft from four different squadrons and shot down six British aircraft flying in smaller formations. Out of these large groups of Albatros, most of the planes painted in bright, colourful designs, emerged what the British later called the 'Richthofen Flying Circus'. But German superiority did not last. Two factors began to turn the situation around in May 1917 for the Royal Flying Corps. British aircraft production was finally reaching significant levels. In January and February the Corps had received 250 new aircraft. In the period March–April the number increased to 612; and in May–June to 757. But it was more than a matter of numbers. The aircraft delivered in late spring represented a new generation of aircraft, the 'fourth generation',

Richthofen's Flying Circus. Jasta 11 Albatros D.III fighters, with the 'Red Baron's' red aircraft second from the front, at Donai on the Western Front in March 1917.

The agile Sopwith F.1 Camel, a British fighter that was deadly to the enemy and demanding on those who flew it. It first reached the Western Front in July 1917 and went on to destroy 1,294 enemy aircraft, more than any other Allied 'Scout'.

as one historian designated them. Aircraft like the Bristol F. 2B, the SE-5a and the Sopwith Camel soon put the German Albatros, even with their better trained aircrews, at a disadvantage.

The decline in British casualties reflected these trends: in April the British suffered 316 casualties among their air crews in approximately 30,000 flying hours of operations over the Western Front. In May the British increased their flying hours by 25 per cent, but saw a drop in casualties to 187; and in June the casualties dropped to 165. With better aircraft and greater numbers the British pressed hard on the German fighter forces, which also had to contend with the French. While the Germans held their own in a defensive sense, they could not match what the British put into the air until early 1918. The creation of the 'Richthofen Flying Circus' – originally based at Courtrai – allowed the Germans to concentrate greater numbers on small sectors of the front than their British opponents did and thus mitigate their growing technological inferiority. In *The Great War in the Air*, John Morrow records that Richthofen himself wrote to a friend in early July: 'You would not believe how low morale is among the fighter pilots presently at the front because of their sorry machines. No one wants to be a fighter pilot any more.' The greatest difficulty the Germans confronted in 1917 was the fact that they were steadily losing the quantitative race to Allied air forces. German industry had done wonders in the quantity and quality of weapons it turned out, and mobilization of German industry had proceeded more quickly than it had with the British. In 1914, the German aviation industry had delivered 1,348 aircraft to the army; in 1915 the number rose to 4,532. But the Germans were confronting a world-wide coalition that, in economic terms, by mid 1915 included the Americans as well.

Throughout 1915 the major powers involved in the war had made a desperate scramble to build up the industrial base for aircraft production, while at the same time coming up with improved designs for the products of that plant. That was an almost impossible task, given how little was known about designing and producing aircraft on a mass production basis. Some national economies and military organizations never solved the problems inherent in wartime aircraft production, the Russian and Austro-Hungarian empires in particular. Yet in Germany and France the results were extraordinary. The Germans produced three times as many aircraft in 1915 as in the year before, along with 5,037 engines. Considering that a substantial portion of their industry was under German control, the French production record in 1915 was even more impressive: 4,489 aircraft and 7,096 engines. The British were less successful, turning out only 1,680 aircraft; moreover, they had to import one third of their engines from the French.

By 1916 order had begun to emerge out of chaos. The growth in workforces was phenomenal. The French expanded from approximately 12,650 workers in the aircraft industry before the war to 30,960 in 1915, and to 68,920 in 1916. The British expansion was even more extraordinary. By August 1916 over 42,000 workers were employed in manufacturing aircraft and engines from an industry which, before the war, had numbered only in the thousands. But that expansion did not come easily; the *laissez-faire* attitudes of the Asquith government resulted in a general lack of a centralized, co-ordinated or even consistent approach to aircraft procurement. It was not until late 1916, with a change of leadership to David Lloyd George, that the British brought some coherence to their procurement programmes.

Nevertheless, in 1916 the British achieved a three-fold increase in aircraft production; but the French still had to supply one third of British engine requirements. The French continued their impressive efforts, although with the usual bickering and arguments. For 1916, they produced 7,549 aircraft, but a truly impressive total of 16,875 engines – of great importance, since their allies were heavily dependent on French imports. Compared with that of the Allies, German production reached its highest point in 1916, when German factories turned out 8,182 aircraft. But the dissonances that marked German aircraft procurement throughout the remainder of the war were already apparent; in 1916 German industry produced only 7,823 engines but, unlike the British, the Germans had no other source. Only the quality of German engines kept the disparity between engine and aircraft production from reaching desperate proportions.

In 1917 the upward surge in production continued, but the pressures on the Germans were telling. The German aircraft industry turned out 13,977 aircraft, a figure that the French more than matched with 14,915. But by now British production had risen too, at 13,766 turning out almost as many aircraft as the Germans. Once again the Germans produced considerably fewer engines, at 12,029, than aircraft. British engine production, at 11,763, was even lower. But French production carried the load for the Allies, with engine production reaching 23,092. Even with the qualitative advantage they enjoyed in the first five months of 1917, the Germans confronted a serious challenge from the

SPAD 13
speed: 128 mph
height: 16,405 ft

Fokker D VII
speed: 125 mph
height: 16,000 ft

BE2–C
speed: 75 mph
height: 10,000 ft

Fokker E1 Eindekker
speed: 81 mph
height: 9,840 ft

Between 1914 and 1918 the performance of both Allied and German 'Scouts', as fighters were known, increased by leaps and bounds. Speed, range, and, most importantly, service ceilings almost doubled, all of which brought new dimensions to air warfare.

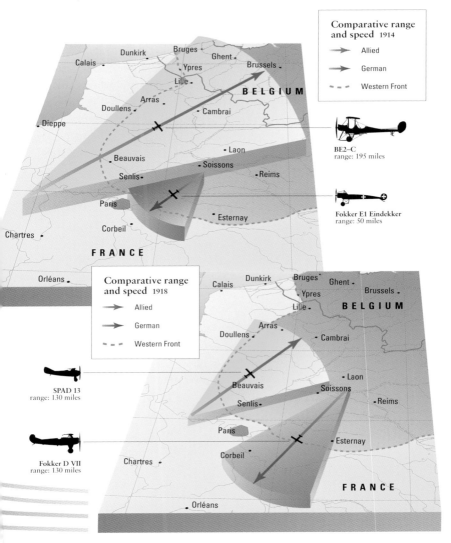

Comparative range and speed 1914

→ Allied

→ German

- - - Western Front

BE2–C
range: 195 miles

Fokker E1 Eindekker
range: 50 miles

Comparative range and speed 1918

→ Allied

→ German

- - - Western Front

SPAD 13
range: 130 miles

Fokker D VII
range: 130 miles

swelling Allied production. But with the British and French regaining the technological edge in the summer, the Germans were in serious trouble. From May 1917, they would be almost entirely on the defensive in the air.

Moreover, at a time when the German high command worried about the possibility of Holland or Denmark entering the war, the new military leadership of Hindenburg and Ludendorff took the extraordinary step of supporting the German navy in its efforts to resume unrestricted submarine warfare in the Atlantic. That action assured the entrance into the war, with its full economic potential, of the United States, although the Somme battle, which the Germans had characterized as the beginning of 'the war of *matériel*', had already underlined the fact that the Reich was falling behind its opponents in the production of war material. Hindenburg and Ludendorff set about repairing the disparity between German production and that of the opposing coalition. As was the case with so much of the German approach to war, the so-called Hindenburg plan set wildly optimistic goals for increasing armaments production, while paying little attention to what was available in terms of raw materials or workforce.

While the Germans discounted the military potential of the United States, they did recognize America's economic potential. Thus, in the early summer of 1917, they set in motion the so-called *Amerikaprogramm* to produce 2,000 aircraft and 2,500 engines per month by January 1918. While such goals were not quite so megalomaniacal as those set by Nazi leaders two decades later, the *Amerikaprogramm* distorted the equilibrium of the aircraft industry. As a result, throughout the remainder of 1917 and into 1918, aircraft prices spiralled upwards, constant strikes occurred throughout German industry and the workmanship declined. Given the fact that aircraft production would not meet its goals, the German air service was faced with Hobson's choice: either robbing its training establishment and aircraft reserve parks to fill up front-line squadrons, or letting front-line strength drop to unacceptable levels. The Germans came nowhere near to achieving their goals; in the first seven months of 1918 they produced barely 1,100 aircraft per month. Moreover, they learned little from their experiences in 1917 and early 1918; having failed to double production in that period, they again planned to double aircraft and engine production by June 1919. Instead military and economic collapse intervened, along with revolution, ending the Reich's war of conquest.

The difficulties under which the German air units were operating showed clearly in summer 1917. In reply to Richthofen's gaggles of aircraft, the British were putting formations of sixty fighters up over Flanders. As the French were in no position to conduct major military operations after the mutinies of May, the Americans remained in general disarray and the Russians were obviously on their way out of the war, the British carried the weight of the Allied effort in summer 1917. Unfortunately, Haig botched things. After the successes of Arras and Messines, there was some reason for optimism. But neither Haig nor his staff had developed a clear understanding of the major changes that were occurring in the tactics of the war. Moreover, with the help of a sycophantic and dysfunctional staff, Haig had lost touch with the sharp end of war. Thus, as his diary underlines, he had little understanding of the catastrophe that enveloped British forces engaged in the battle of Passchendaele. By 1917 the BEF had not yet reached a level of tactical sophistication which would bring great operational success. But Haig exacerbated the BEF's weaknesses by picking a location (Flanders) and a time of year when weather and geography made prospects hopeless.

On 1 August 1917 – after two weeks' preliminary bombardment that thoroughly alerted the Germans – the British threw their forces (as well as those of the Dominions) into a meat-grinder battle, the conditions of which were unimaginable except to those who were engaged in it. Haig's chief of staff, Lancelot Kiggell, exclaimed in November after visiting the front lines for the first time, 'My God, did we send men to fight in that?' The conditions of the battle minimized the changes in artillery that emphasized indirect controlled fire, as well as the potential of the Royal Flying Corps, despite its improvements in both its quantity and its quality.

When weather conditions in Flanders were suitable, British aircraft carried out attacks on targets in the German rear areas – airfields, railroad stations and trains. They also attacked German front-line positions directly. British ground-attack aircrews were not as well trained or prepared as their German counterparts. Given a flying speed of approximately 100 mph, the casualties from German ground fire were high. Arthur Lee was the only one of three flight commanders left within a week after his squadron began such attacks. He himself was shot down on three out of his first seven sorties, but in each case crash-landed his shot-up aircraft within British lines.

With the dismal failure at Passchendaele Haig was in serious political trouble at home. Perhaps for this reason, perhaps because he had been a great supporter of tank development throughout the war, in late November 1917 Haig authorized an attack at Cambrai that relied heavily on the tank. There would be no preliminary bombardment; rather, the planners relied on the tanks and a heavy bombardment just prior to zero-hour to get the infantry across the killing zone and into the enemy's defensive system. The attack succeeded beyond Haig's wildest expectations. In one day it gained as much territory as the Passchendaele offensive had captured in three-and-a-half months. DH 5s directly supported the tanks, attacking German artillery positions which threatened the advancing tanks, while attack aircraft severely impeded German defensive efforts even when the tanks had broken down or been destroyed.

One week later a German counter-attack drove the British back from their gains with a well-executed, combined-arms, infantry-artillery attack based on exploitation, initiative and speed. Here again, close air-support aircraft substantially aided the Germans. In this case, some of the German aircraft were the new Junkers J.I, an all-metal, armoured attack aircraft the Junkers firm had designed especially for the ground-support mission. The German counter-offensive, based on tactical rather than technological innovation, underlined how the pace of innovation on the Western Front had picked up since the war's early years. In effect the Germans were on the way to inventing modern warfare.

1918: THE LAST YEAR

With the Russian collapse in 1917 and an offensive in October that nearly destroyed the Italian armed forces, the Germans possessed a window of opportunity to break the Western Front before the weight of US armament production and military forces could make themselves felt. There was, of course, an alternative strategy the Germans might have pursued, given the serious political and economic situation back home: a compromise peace in the west that allowed the Reich to keep some of its massive acquisitions in the east. But Ludendorff had no intention of settling for half a loaf when he could have a long shot at gaining everything.

Thus the Germans determined to launch a great offensive on the Western Front in March 1918. Because of substantial morale problems in that theatre due to Bolshevik propaganda, they deployed few troops from the east for the attack. Instead, the German high command placed its trust on revolutionary new tactics that depended on surprise, highly

The SE-5a was considered by many as the best British fighter of the First World War. SE-5as of 29 Squadron are seen here in front of their French Besonneau canvas hangars at St Omer on the Western Front in 1918, a few days after the formation of the Royal Air Force.

accurate, sudden artillery bombardments aimed at disrupting the enemy's equilibrium rather than destroying his forces entirely, and rapid exploitation of any and all tactical advantages.

Operation Michael, the code name for the offensive, commenced on 21 March 1918. Using skilful and disciplined deployment, the Germans concentrated a large number of artillery pieces and a considerable number of aircraft against the British Third and Fifth Armies. The Germans had 3,668 aircraft in the west, as against only 2,271 the previous year. Particularly against the Fifth Army the German attack achieved a stunning success, ripping the British defensive line to shreds. British co-operation between air units and the artillery broke down in foggy conditions and under the weight of the German attack.

For the first two days German aircraft dominated the skies over their rapidly advancing forces. But by 24 March reinforcing Allied air units had moved to support the Third Army and the disintegrating divisions of the Fifth Army. These aerial reinforcements caused severe casualties to German ground and air forces. Both sides threw their air forces into the battle, regardless of the casualties, to attack enemy ground forces, and the losses in air units were high. By the end of the month the German advance had captured an astonishing amount of territory for a First World War offensive, but in a strategic and operational sense the Germans were the losers. They now had a much longer front to defend, one which was, moreover, weaker defensively.

The March offensive presaged a number of German offensives that lasted into early June; some were notably successful in driving the Allies back and seizing territory. But none gained significant operational objectives, and all were immensely costly. Between March and July the Germans suffered nearly 1,000,000 casualties, far more than at Verdun, the Somme or Passchendaele. Casualties in the air were equally heavy. Even in January, before the attacks began, the German air service suffered a loss of 779 aircraft and 241 aircrew out of 4,500 on the Western Front (approximately a 6 per cent loss rate). By May the German air service was losing one seventh of its pilots every month – a burden which the training establishment could not support. At the end of April, shortly after he had recorded his eightieth kill, the redoubtable Richthofen fell victim to the guns of Captain Roy Brown or to Australian anti-aircraft gunners on the ground.

By now, both sides were devoting considerable resources to night bombing. The reason for this had much to do with the heavy casualties suffered by bombers in daylight raids. Results were mixed; undoubtedly night-time raids were a great annoyance to the enemy, but the damage inflicted was minimal unless attacks occurred during periods of full moon and clear weather. For the most part, such attacks simply scattered bombs over the landscape. As one British bomber pilot observed in 1917, 'Experience has shown that it is quite easy for five squadrons to set out to bomb a particular target and for only one of those five ever to reach the objective; while the other four, in the honest belief that they have done so, have bombed four different villages which bore little, if any, resemblance to the one they desired to attack.'

The result of the pressure Allied air forces placed on the German air service was a steady deterioration of air support for German ground forces during the climactic summer battles. Despite the arrival of an

The German Gotha G III bomber replaced the Zeppelin airships which were far too vulnerable when used for air raids on London. The first mass bombing raid on England by Gotha bombers was made on 25 May 1917, when twenty-one aircraft attacked towns in south-east England, killing ninety-five people and injuring many more.

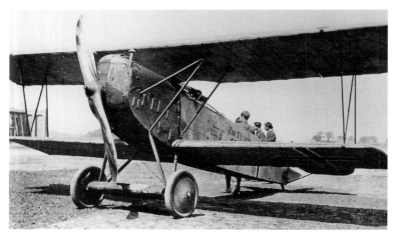

Recognized as one of the best single-seat 'Scouts' of the First World War, the Fokker D.VII first entered service in May 1918. Although it eventually replaced all other German fighters on the Western Front, it arrived too late to relieve Allied pressure on German forces.

excellent new fighter aircraft, the Fokker D.VII, which, as historian John Morrow has noted, had the ability 'to make a good pilot out of mediocre material', the German air service made less and less of a contribution to the battle on the ground. The numbers against the Germans and the pressures of constant Allied offensives were too much. Moreover, the Germans could not make good the losses they had suffered in their spring attacks, especially with regard to pilots.

On 8 August 1918 the British and Australian troops gained a signal success over the Germans. After a short sudden bombardment that had smashed the main defences identified by aerial photographs, massed tanks, supported by close air-support strikes, got the infantry across the killing zone and through the German defences – a success that Ludendorff termed the 'blackest day of the war for the German army'. Yet German aircraft prevented Allied bombers from destroying the Somme bridges and inflicted heavy casualties on the attackers. But the fact that the British and French concentrated 1,904 aircraft (988 fighters) on a twenty-five-mile front against only 365 German aircraft (140 fighters) underlines the kinds of odds the Germans now confronted.

Increasing numbers of British, French and American aircraft (the Americans flying French and British products) harried the Germans across the Western Front. Moreover, there were few easy kills for the Germans. The British had finally established a sensible training programme that prepared fighter and support pilots for the ferocious fighting environment of the Western Front. And the Americans, generally unwilling to learn from the experiences of their Allies, at least proved willing to listen when it came to the training of pilots and aircrew. At the start of their spring offensive in March 1918 the German air service had possessed 3,668 combat aircraft; by November it was down to 2,709 combat aircraft, a 27 per cent drop in fighting strength; the decline in experience among the fighter pilots was even greater, given the enormous losses the Germans had suffered.

Admittedly, the Germans never entirely lost their ability to inflict casualties, as the Americans discovered in their attack on the St Mihiel salient. The US 1st Day Bombardment Group lost thirty-one pilots and observers, sixteen from one squadron alone, in the first four days of the offensive. But the Germans were decreasingly able to affect the ground situation. German reconnaissance aircraft rarely obtained a coherent picture of what was happening on the other side of the lines; German balloon operations were virtually shut down by aggressive attacks, especially by the Americans. The American ace Frank Luke made it his specialty to attack balloons; in an eighteen-day period he destroyed seventeen, despite intensive anti-aircraft fire. German air units now had to pull back rapidly to less well-equipped bases as Allied offensives lashed their army back into Belgium. Even the new airfields came under intense attack, while transportation difficulties made it increasingly difficult to get fuel supplies to air units fighting in the west; some German fighter squadrons were limited to ten flights a day during the critical summer months.

Production numbers for the three major powers underline the hopeless position strategic over-extension had created for their air services. In 1918, despite massive efforts to create a command economy

Captain Arthur 'Ray' R. Brooks, 22nd Aero Squadron pilot, with his Spad S.13 with which he shot down a total of six enemy aircraft in 1918. He flew with the USAAC during the Second World War and died in 1991 of old age.

that turned out 2,000 aircraft per month, the Germans fell well short of their goal. Desperate efforts did get aircraft production to 2,000 in October for the first time, but that figure was more than offset by the overwhelming production advantage the Allies enjoyed. Thus the Germans ended up with a net minus because their losses were by now so great. Production figures for 1918 underlined the trends that had developed since 1914. In the first seven months of 1918 German aircraft firms turned out only 8,055 aircraft and 9,050 engines, compared to the French, who turned out 24,652 aircraft and 44,563 engines in the year. The British showed an astonishing improvement in 1918, a reflection of Lloyd George's effective and thorough mobilization of Britain's industry and resources, British firms doubling their production from 1917 by turning out 30,761 aircraft (plus an additional 1,865 seaplanes). The success was not quite so striking in engine production, with 22,088, again supplemented by engines imported from France.

The great disappointment was the American failure to get a single fighter aircraft of their own production into combat. That would undoubtedly have changed in 1919, but it represented a dismal record, especially given the boastful claims the Americans had made when they entered the war. The major cause of the US failure had to do with the general unwillingness of the Wilson administration to prepare the industrial base for armament production before the United States entered the war. This particularly affected aircraft production. But the young assistant secretary of the navy, one Franklin Delano Roosevelt, watched the botched aircraft programmes and twenty years later ensured that his administration set in motion a major expansion of the industrial base for aircraft production well *before* the United States entered that war.

STRATEGIC BOMBING

In November 1914, the German Grand Admiral, Alfred von Tirpitz, creator of the High Sea Fleet, noted in a letter to a friend that the first Zeppelin raids on England had terrified the English, but that he was not in favour of 'frightfulness ... [S]ingle bombs from flying machines are wrong; they are odious when they hit and kill old women, and one gets used to them. If [however] one could set fire to London in thirty places, then what in a small way is odious would retire before something fine and powerful.' Tirpitz's comments encapsulate what was to be at the heart of strategic bombing in the First World War: the difficulty in moving from the ability to kill or maim relatively small numbers of individuals to the ability to inflict substantial damage that would interfere with the enemy's capacity to wage war.

Given their enthusiasm for *Schrechlichkeit* (frightfulness), the Germans were the most enthusiastic and consistent in their pursuit of strategic bombing. However, all the major powers involved in the air war in the west pursued strategic bombing to some degree. Even the Italians devoted substantial resources to creating a bomber fleet that could extend the war beyond the innumerable, fruitless battles along the Isonzo. Part of this effort to create strategic bombing capabilities resulted from a desperate desire to escape the hideous slaughter of the trenches and the frustration at what seemed to be a war with no foreseeable end and few successes. But strategic bombing was also

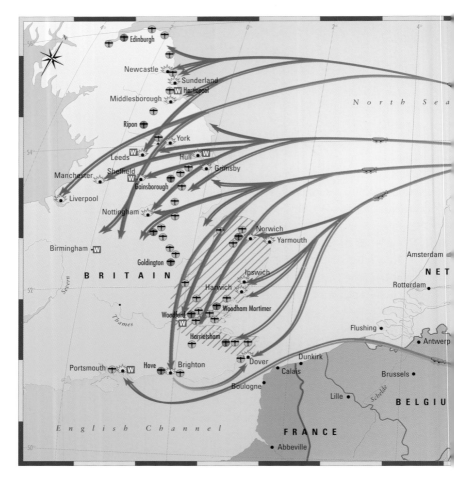

attractive to a mind-set which believed that civilian society, particularly the working class, had been softened and weakened as a result of the industrial age. By striking directly at the working class, air power could attack the enemy's soft underbelly.

The Germans, however, enjoyed one luxury their opponents did not. Both London and Paris were relatively close to German air bases located on the territory acquired in the 1914 advance of German troops. Berlin or even the Ruhr, on the other hand, were quite distant from Allied air bases. As the Tirpitz quotation above suggests, the

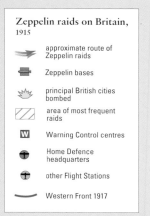

WAR COMES TO THE
HOME FRONT
*On 19 January 1915 three
Imperial German Navy Airship
Division Zeppelins made their
first bombing raid on the British
Isles, killing two people and
injuring thirteen in King's Lynn,
Norfolk. More than a hundred
German army and navy
Zeppelin airships bombed
British targets, the last on
6 August 1918.*

Germans launched their effort in late 1914 with Zeppelin attacks. Most of these attacks occurred at night. Even though the Germans did not lose their first Zeppelin to a British night fighter until early September 1916, the dirigibles caused only minor damage.

But by then, with a considerable investment, the Germans were preparing a force of 'heavy' bombers, the Gothas, for deployment in north-western Belgium. Two Mercedes engines could get the Gotha bombers up to 12,000 feet, where they cruised along at a majestic speed of 80 mph; given the distances they had to fly and the technology available, bomb loads rarely exceeded 1,000 pounds. The first raid in late May 1917 targeted London, but ran into heavy cumulus clouds. The bomber formation then turned south-east and attacked Folkestone on its return to Belgium. Part of the bomb load hit a crowded shopping arcade and killed 95 people, wounding 260. Given the island nation's traditional sense of security, there was great outrage in the press. A week later the Germans were back; this time they hit Liverpool Street Station and a nursery school as well. Casualties were 162 dead and 432 wounded. In response to the public outcry, the Cabinet ordered two fighter squadrons to return from France, despite the protests of Trenchard and Haig.

When Gothas bombed the East End, less than two weeks later, one of the fighter squadrons was already back in France. So far British defence measures had been ineffectual, but in the next three raids

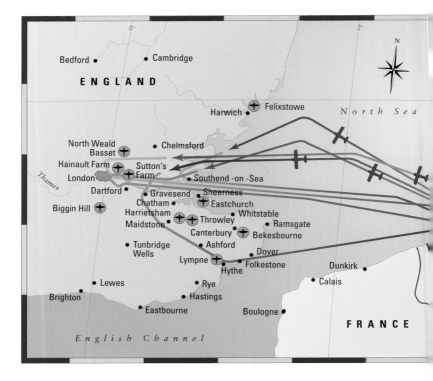

British fighters shot down four bombers, and five German planes crashed without any help from the defence force. In effect the result was that these three missions cost the Germans nearly a third of their 'heavy' bombers. Nevertheless, there was uproar in British political circles, which resulted in the establishment of a committee under Jan Smuts, the South African statesman, to study the problem and, eventually, the creation of the Royal Air Force. The German attacks also led to the creation of an effective air-defence system that presaged the system (but not of course the radar) that defended the United Kingdom during the Battle of Britain.

The Germans were sufficiently impressed by the growing effectiveness of British defences to move to night attacks. One attack by full moon hit a barracks at Chatham Dockyards and killed 131 sailors, injuring 90 others. But British night defences also improved, after some disorganization at the beginning. During the night of 28 September 1917 British defenders shot down four bombers, while the Germans themselves crashed five

The Gotha Raids 25 May–12 August 1917

→	25 May	✚	British airfield
→	13 June	✚	German airfield
→	7 July	—	Western Front
→	12 August	▨	German occupied territory

GERMAN HEAVY BOMBERS
Germany was the first to recognize the potential of the heavy bomber. By the summer of 1917 twin-engine Gotha bombers, which could carry a 900-pound bomb load, were carrying out a series of night raids on British cities, causing considerable damage and civilian casualties.

more. The Germans now added incendiaries to their loads. On 6 December Gothas dropped ten tons of bombs over London, but the London Fire Brigade's rapid responses kept damage to a relatively low level.

Twelve days later the Germans struck Britain again and, while they damaged a considerable amount of property, they killed only twelve civilians. Out of thirteen aircraft, the Germans lost only one to a British fighter, but they wrecked eight of the aircraft themselves on return. As was to be the case in the Second World War as well, British anti-aircraft guns expended huge amounts of ammunition to little purpose. But the creation of a defensive scheme of reporting, anti-aircraft guns, balloons and night fighters presented the Germans with a real air-defence system. The last German raid over the night of 19–20 May 1918 saw twenty-eight Gothas and three Giant bombers attack various targets. But British night fighters shot down three, and anti-aircraft guns accounted for another three. The 20 per cent casualty rate persuaded the German high command to end the bombing campaign.

What had the Germans achieved? Not much, except to persuade the British to stick it out to the end. But the bombing did contribute directly to the creation of the Royal Air Force as a separate service. The public outcry also had considerable impact on Trenchard's thinking. After a short but unsuccessful stint as the RAF's first chief of staff, Trenchard returned to France in the summer of 1918 to command the long-range bomber force that the British were establishing to strike back at the Germans. That force attacked a number of German towns in the fall, but its losses were high and the material effects disappointing. Nevertheless, this did not prevent the Air Ministry from claiming in October 1918 that 'though material damage is as yet slight when compared with the moral effect, it is certain that the destruction of "morale" will start before the destruction of factories and, consequently, loss of production will precede material damage'.

THE WAR IN THE AIR

At the beginning of the First World War aircraft represented a weapon of great promise but of minimal performance. Had the war been of short duration, the aeroplane would have received little attention because of its minimal contribution, and its development would have continued at a leisurely, casual pace. But the stalemate on the ground created an enormous demand for aircraft for reconnaissance and artillery spotting. The importance of those roles to the fighting on the ground quickly and inevitably led the opponents to contest the air over the trenches in order to protect their own reconnaissance aircraft and attack those of the enemy.

The resulting struggle for control of the air began in earnest in late 1915 and continued unabated to the end of the war. The cost of that struggle in terms of aircrew and aircraft led to demands for immediate and drastic improvements in the quantity as well as the quality of aircraft. The result was dramatic improvements in aircraft and engine performance, and in aircrew proficiency, and hence an increase in the importance of aircraft to the battle below. As the French discovered in April 1917, the loss of control of the air had a disastrous impact on the battle along the Chemin des Dames.

The length and devastating casualties of the war forced the growing air services to consider using aircraft to attack the enemy's rear areas; some even saw aircraft as a means to attack the enemy's population and industrial base, the battlefront's main support. For this, technology presented huge difficulties, as the means and capabilities to wage an effective strategic bombing campaign were not yet available. But here too the airmen of the First World War had charted the way to the future.

In sum, the First World War had resulted in the creation, at great cost and suffering, of modern war. And for that, what had happened in the air was as important as what had occurred on the ground. After 1918 war between the major powers was inconceivable without the aeroplane, and all the wishful thinking in the 1920s and 1930s could not put the genie back in its bottle.

CHAPTER TWO

The Interwar Years

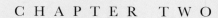

Deutschland über alles: *Germany's latest trans-Atlantic airship* Hindenburg *with Nazi swastikas prominent on its fins, flies over the skyscrapers of New York in 1936.*

The Interwar Years

THE TREATY OF VERSAILLES concluded 'the war to end wars' on a most unsatisfactory note. It imposed severe penalties on the Germans, one of which banned the Reich from possessing military aircraft. With hindsight the settlement fell between two stools – it was not harsh enough to prevent the Germans from attempting to regain their position, but not pacific enough to win their support for the established order. France's Marshal Ferdinand Foch suggested, all too accurately, that the treaty was only a twenty-year truce. But in 1919 few people in Europe felt that way.

One of the clearer lessons of the war was that the aeroplane was an essential component in the military equation. The difficulty in continuing post-war aircraft development was that while the aeroplane represented considerable military potential, the state of the technology was not yet adequate for civilian applications, since the aeroplane offered little by way of range, load-carrying capacity or passenger safety. Militarily, severe retrenchments even in the forces of the

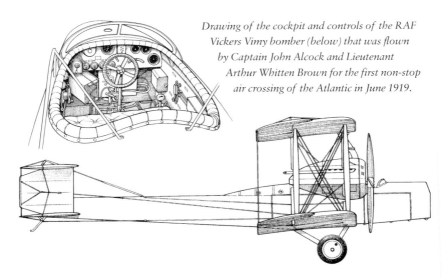

Drawing of the cockpit and controls of the RAF Vickers Vimy bomber (below) that was flown by Captain John Alcock and Lieutenant Arthur Whitten Brown for the first non-stop air crossing of the Atlantic in June 1919.

victorious powers meant that resources for research and development, or even for the maintenance of standing air forces, were limited. As a result there was a lack of funding from either governments or industry to further the development of aircraft technology. The onset of the Depression in 1929 only exacerbated this state of affairs.

Nevertheless, there was great enthusiasm for the potential of aircraft within military organizations as well as in the civilian world. Prizes were offered and meets held; competition for record-breaking flights received great publicity; and the aeroplane received as much attention from the public as it had during the war, if not more. Considerable acclaim in both America and Europe greeted Charles Lindbergh's solo flight across the Atlantic. On a smaller scale, barnstormers were worshipped in every small American field from which they flew. Public interest in flight supported much of the technological development that took place through to the mid 1930s, but it was scarcely enough to support major research and developmental efforts to further aircraft or engine technology.

As they were forbidden military and multi-engine aircraft in the early 1920s, the Germans pursued gliders with a passion that attempted to recapture the romance of air-to-air combat in the First World War. As Peter Fritzsche notes in *A Nation of Fliers*, the monument to First World War German fliers on the Wasserkuppe, the centre of gliding in the Weimar Republic, overlooked the open fields below and bore an inscription that skated over the depressing present (at least in terms of German air power) and linked the military past to a glowing future: 'We dead fliers/Remain victors/By our own efforts/Volk fly again/And you will become a victor/By your own effort.'

DEVELOPING THEORIES OF AIR POWER

Much of the debate about the potential of aircraft took place within military organizations. There were several lessons that should have been clear from the experiences of the war. First was the absolute requirement for air superiority before aircraft could accomplish other operations without suffering unacceptable losses. Second, whatever advantages aircraft offered in attacking far behind the enemy's lines – and hence restoring a certain mobility to war – there were great difficulties not only in hitting targets accurately, but in judging the effects of those attacks on material and morale.

The impact of aircraft in the First World War created a considerable group of enthusiasts within military organizations. By and large they saw air power in terms of its potential in future conflicts. These advocates of air power saw the aircraft as a means to escape the slaughter of the trenches. They were also undoubtedly influenced by the heavy casualties air units had suffered in supporting the ground forces in the terrible battles of attrition on the Western Front, and this experience led almost inevitably to a belief that the future of air power lay in a service which would be independent of the constraints imposed by ground and naval officers. Consequently, much of the discussion about air power in the interwar period focused on whether an independent service should be formed.

In the case of Britain, which had already created an independent service (the Royal Air Force) in the First World War, such arguments revolved around the continued independence of that service. In the United States, on the other hand, the debate centred on whether an independent air service should be created. The Germans, of course, given Versailles, did not have to confront the problem in the 1920s; perhaps for this reason, their approach to air power was to become the most reasonable and analytical. The intellectual and doctrinal arguments taking place within the militaries of the major powers exercised a dominant influence over the choice and conduct of air war in the coming conflict. Since none of the participants possessed our knowledge of what air war in the future might look like, the ways in which the different military organizations prepared for the next conflict reveals much about the processes of change in an uncertain and complex environment.

At the start of the twenty-first century the Italian air-power thinker Giulio Douhet enjoys an undeserved reputation as a premier theorist of the interwar period. Douhet certainly exercised considerable influence in Italy, but there is little evidence that he influenced the development of interwar air doctrine or theories in Britain, for example. After the Second World War, Arthur Harris, the leader of Bomber Command for much of the war, was entirely dismissive of the idea that anyone in the Royal Air Force had ever read a book by 'an Italian', much less been influenced by one. On the other hand, the Italian military attaché in

Policing the Empire. An Indian-based RAF Hawker Hart light bomber of 39 Squadron in the 1930s flying over the 22,000ft peak of Nanga Parbat in the Himalayas, without the aid of oxygen, with Mount Everest in the background.

Washington did make some of Douhet's writings available to the Americans in translation in the late 1920s and early 1930s.

Above all Douhet's arguments were symptomatic of the theories of air power which dominated the interwar period, particularly in Britain and the United States. Put simply, Douhet argued for propositions largely derived from his understanding of where technology was going; they certainly did not derive from an analysis of the air war in the First World War. There was a superficial set of 'larger' lessons to which Douhet could point. Certainly, military operations on the Western Front suggested that any future war involving large ground forces would be inordinately costly in lives and treasure. Moreover, the First World War had also indicated that virtually everything – industry, cities, transportation, workers and innocent civilians – would be open to attack in the next conflict.

With these principles in mind, Douhet argued that air power could reach across the battlefield and attack the enemy's homeland directly. Through a combination of high explosives, incendiaries and gas bombs, he argued, air attacks could break the enemy's will at the outset of war. Such a possibility demanded an almost exclusive focus on strategic bombing. Moreover, Douhet argued that there was little possibility of intercepting attacking bombers with fighter planes. In effect, the British politician Stanley Baldwin was echoing Douhet's arguments of the early 1930s when he told the House of Commons that 'the bomber will always get through'.

Such theories of strategic bombing involved an explicit rejection of history. In 1924 the British air staff noted in a memorandum to the Cabinet that, in war, air forces could

'either bomb military objectives in populated areas from the beginning of the war, with the objective of obtaining a decision by moral effect which such attacks will produce, and by the serious dislocation of the normal life of the country, or, alternatively, they can be used in the first instance to attack enemy aerodromes with a view to gaining some measure of air superiority and, when this has been gained, can be changed over to the direct attack of the nation. The latter alternative is the method that the lessons of military history seem to recommend, but the Air Staff are convinced that the former is the correct one.'

Thus air-power theories rejected not only the traditional lessons of military history, but even the combat lessons of the last war.

As with so much military thinking in the early years of the twentieth century, air power advocates believed that the staying power of civilians in any nation at war was far less than that of the military institutions defending the nation. Again, this was an explicit rejection of the First World War's experience: the French army, not the nation, had come close to collapse in 1917; in Germany it had been first the navy and then the army that had spearheaded revolution in 1918. Nevertheless, in discussion with his subordinates about a possible war with France, Lord Trenchard, the RAF's chief of air staff in the 1920s, argued that 'I feel that although there would be an outcry, the French in a bombing duel would probably squeal before we did. That was really the first thing. The nation that would stand being bombed longest would win in the end.'

Douhet's approach (and that of most other air-power theorists) represented the hope that air power – in the guise of strategic bombing – would return war to the era of short, decisive conflicts. Thus, it would allow Europe to escape the endless slaughter of the last war. However, nowhere in Douhet's writings was there a sense of the technological and industrial underpinnings that air war had and would require in the future. This may have reflected the particular weaknesses of Italy, since that nation possessed few of the resources and little of the expertise or industrial strength required for air war. Yet most other air power theorists of the period were similarly reluctant to recognize these requirements.

Finally, what makes the conventional wisdom about theories of air power in the 1920s and 1930s so surprising is that these theories belittled the importance of all the major functions of air forces except, of course, strategic bombing. They wrote off air defence, air superiority, interdiction, close air support, and reconnaissance and naval air arms as detracting from the true purpose of air power. The air forces of Great Britain and the United States would pay a substantial penalty at the beginning of the Second World War for their enthusiastic acceptance of such assumptions.

NATIONAL DEVELOPMENTS: BRITAIN

The RAF's interwar development was masterminded by Sir Hugh Trenchard. In a political environment of benign neglect and with severe constraints on the funding of defence, the RAF found itself under direct attack from the army and the navy in the 1920s. Trenchard, consequently, confronted the problem of justifying the RAF's existence. His approach to these attacks lay in a strident offensive, arguing that strategic bombing was the *raison d'être* of the RAF and that such an approach offered Britain security in a troubled and uncertain world. This concept of strategic bombing would dominate much of the RAF's preparation for and conduct of the next war.

Trenchard's role and influence has received considerable negative attention from historians, because of his almost exclusive focus on strategic bombing. However, he undoubtedly saved the RAF as a separate military organization. Whatever the deficiencies in his conception of air power, it is likely that the Royal Navy or the army would have minimized air power's potential to an even greater extent. Moreover, Trenchard proved himself an outstanding developer of talent. In the 1930s the RAF produced an exceptional group of airmen, among whom were Hugh Dowding, Arthur Tedder, John Slessor and Arthur Harris. Trenchard also possessed considerable political astuteness. The RAF might argue in favour of strategic bombing, but in the meantime its squadrons were playing an important role in colonial policing. In the war's aftermath, the British had assumed long-term control of Iraq; there the RAF put down a tribal revolt at considerably

A flight of RAF Hawker Fury Mk 1 fighters of No 1 Squadron's aerobatic team of 1937–8 led by Flt. Lt E. M. Donaldson, who would later become a Battle of Britain ace.

less cost than would have been incurred if ground forces had been used. Equally important was the RAF's role in mapping and executing aerial reconnaissance of the empire's wide expanses, especially in Africa. Finally, during the 1920s, Trenchard spent a considerable portion of the RAF's budget on building the infrastructure and airfields which would prove essential to the service's expansion in the late 1930s and during the Second World War.

In the 1930s the British confronted the German threat once again, this time in the form of a ferocious ideology, one that aimed not just at minor alterations in the European balance, but quite literally at its destruction. Britain's strategic and economic difficulties only served to exacerbate the unease the British felt in confronting another war. Threatened in the Far East by Japan, in the Mediterranean by the Italians and on the continent by Germany, the British temporized with a policy of appeasement. Air power played an increasingly important part in the diplomatic equation because of the fears it aroused in British leaders as to the vulnerability of their nation.

Of the three services, the RAF received a greater share of the resources an unwilling government made available, but that is not saying much. Ill-thought-out expansion plans followed one after another. At the end of 1937 the Chamberlain government refused financial support for the large-scale production of bombers, but it did not, as some have suggested, increase the funding for fighters either. Had it done so, it might have exercised some considerable impact on air operations in the 1940 campaign in the Low Countries. In 1938, British fortunes reached a nadir in both foreign and defence policies.

Chamberlain's sacrifice of Czechoslovakia at Munich in September 1938 reflected less the fear that Britain would lose a war – remarks made at the time indicate that Chamberlain believed that Britain would win – but rather the cost in human and material terms of such a war to Britain, particularly with London's vulnerability to air attack. The government's greatest strategic error in 1938 was not necessarily Munich, but rather its refusal to increase defence spending significantly after September 1938. Instead the appeasers temporized, and there was no substantial increase in defence spending even with regards to air defence. The government did increase the number of fighters on order by 300, but only by extending contracts from 1940 through 1941; in other words it ordered no additional aircraft for the immediate future. It was not until the seizure of the remainder of Czechoslovakia in March 1939 by the German army that the British seriously altered their priorities in allocating resources to defence; by then it was too late for almost everyone except Fighter Command.

If the appeasers left much to be desired on the strategic level, the RAF's preparations for the war were no more enlightened. The air staff proved unimaginative and unwilling to recognize substantive problems. For the most part, senior air leaders held fast to Trenchard's ideological belief in the bomber. This approach rejected co-operation with the other services. Despite the fact that the First World War had underlined the crucial importance of air power to the war against the submarine, the RAF proved disinterested in supporting Coastal Command. Similarly, the RAF put few resources into developing aircraft for the Royal Navy for operations off aircraft carriers. Thus, while the Royal Naval Air Service had pioneered the development of aircraft carriers in the First World War, the British lost their technological and operational lead in the interwar period to the Americans and the Japanese. An acrimonious quarrel between the two services lasted until the late 1930s and played a major role in hindering British effectiveness in carrier warfare. The RAF's relations with the army were even worse; a manoeuvre in the summer of 1939 led a disgusted Archibald Wavell to note that the RAF had done nothing to prepare itself to support ground forces in the field.

The most astonishing aspect of the RAF in the interwar period is that it did little to prepare itself even for the one role on which it believed it should concentrate: strategic bombing. The RAF certainly had evidence that its bombers had substantial problems with navigation and bombing accuracy in the 1930s. In May 1938 the assistant chief of air staff admitted that 'in the home defence exercise last year, bombing accuracy was very poor indeed. Investigation into this matter indicates that this was probably due very largely to the failure to identify targets rather than to fatigue.' Admittedly, rapid expansion and inadequate equipment led commanders to focus training during periods of daylight and good weather in order to hold down accidents – a factor which only reinforced the inability to recognize the weaknesses in the bomber forces.

The Air Ministry did create an advisory board to look into scientific problems associated with bomber operations, but the committee worked directly for an air staff that – removed as it was from day-to-day operations – did not really believe there was a problem. Most of the committee's recommendations and proposals were filtered out before reaching Bomber Command, a command, moreover, which proved itself generally disinterested in technology or in recognizing problems. The result was that, while in September 1939 German bombers possessed navigational and blind-bombing devices, Bomber Command did not receive similar technological aids until 1942. In the meantime, RAF bomber crews had to navigate through the skies over Nazi Germany 'by guess and by God'. Thus much of the British bombing effort in the war's first years went into killing cows and blowing up trees.

Equally astonishing in terms of its technological reductionism was a belief by many in the Air Ministry and in Bomber Command that long-range escort fighters were not only not needed, but unfeasible. In 1941 Churchill asked the chief of air staff, Sir Charles Portal, whether it might not be possible to build fighters to accompany and protect bombers deep into Germany. Portal replied, with absolute assurance, that such fighter aircraft were an impossibility. As Churchill underlined, such a view 'closed many doors'.

Fighter Command stands in startling contrast with what occurred in the rest of the RAF. Here the presence of Sir Hugh Dowding, one of the great innovators of the interwar period, made a crucial difference to technological and operational innovation. In the interwar period Dowding had made a name for himself as a competent administrator and organizer, but he was not an inspiring leader. Nevertheless, in the early 1930s he assumed control of the RAF's research and development efforts. One of his early decisions set the specifications for designs that would eventually turn into the Hurricane and Spitfire. But Dowding is best remembered for his support of experiments in using radio waves to locate aircraft. As Alan Beyerchen has commented:

Dowding was indisputably the pivotal military figure [in regard to radar's development], providing the pull toward new operational developments and innovation. He took a strong personal interest in radar research and development and even flew in the research aircraft to see the project's progress for himself. He also insisted that military personnel be posted right with the 'Boffins' ... This ensured that the RAF personnel actually understood what was happening and that the civilians could be kept aware of military constraints and needs.

Hawker Hurricane Mk 1 fighters of 'Treble One' Squadron seen at RAF Northolt in 1938 temporarily wearing the numbers '111' painted on the camouflaged aircraft.

In 1937 Dowding lost out in the selection process for a new chief of air staff. Instead he received command of Fighter Command, a new home defence organization, established to meet the threat of the rapidly expanding Luftwaffe. Nothing could have been more fortuitous for Britain's long-range security. Having established the technological parameters which would form the basis of his command's fighting power, Dowding proceeded to integrate that technology into a fighting command. He had some help in that the British had developed an effective system of air defence in the First World War (within the limits of the available technology), the system that had defeated the Gotha attacks on London (see above). Dowding saw technological developments as a means to improve that system as opposed to an entirely new way of fighting. The British approach stands in considerable contrast to the Luftwaffe's use of radar, where the Germans saw radar as a technological device that could operate on its own and allow considerable manpower savings.

By summer 1939 Dowding and his subordinates had developed a full-blown system of air defence. There were considerable difficulties between 1937, when he assumed command, and 1939. Particularly in summer and autumn 1938, as the new Hurricanes and Spitfires arrived in the squadrons, Fighter Command ran into major problems with accidents and low rates of operational readiness, which can be attributed to the difficulties involved in introducing the new aircraft. But by September 1939, Fighter Command, alone of the RAF's forces, was ready for war.

THE AMERICANS

During the interwar period American air-power advocates developed ideas similar to those held by their counterparts in Britain. The similarities resulted from the fact that enemy ground and naval forces never significantly threatened the homeland. But in the case of the United States the ideologues of air power failed to gain complete control over air matters. The result was that arguments over air power revolved around efforts to create an independent air service, prevented by the skilful arguments of the US Navy.

William 'Billy' Mitchell has come to epitomize the struggle of American airmen to gain their independence. However, there are a number of interesting aspects to the Mitchell story that do not usually receive attention from the panegyrists. First, Mitchell was more than a strategic bombing advocate. He argued for a balanced air force, one that would contain at least 60 per cent fighters. He believed that the enemy's air force should be the primary target at the outset of war and that one could not begin extensive bombing until one had gained air superiority. In this respect his views stood in the opposite corner from those of Douhet and Trenchard. In fact, his views represented a distillation of what combat experience in the First World War suggested about the future of war in the air.

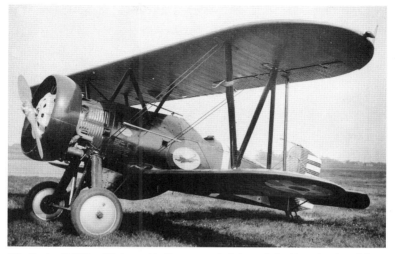

The Boeing B-12D, a US Army Air Corps pursuit fighter of the 1930s developed from the US Navy's F4B-1 carrier-borne fighters, remained in service as an advanced trainer until the outbreak of the Second World War.

In other respects, however, Mitchell agreed with British thinking. Like Douhet, Trenchard believed that air power had rendered armies and navies irrelevant to the conduct of war. Initially Mitchell co-operated with and supported naval reformers and advocated greater emphasis on naval air power. But as he grew more insistent, he increasingly targeted naval air power as well as the admirals in his well-publicized attacks. These attacks culminated in a diatribe about 'the incompetency, criminal negligence, and almost treasonable administration of national defence', shortly after the destruction of the navy dirigible *Shenandoah* in a thunderstorm. The result, not surprisingly, was a court martial in 1925. Found guilty, Mitchell's sentence was mild (a five year suspension from active duty), but he resigned from the army anyway. He was hardly a martyr, since no military organization could possibly have tolerated the barbs he launched at his superiors. Indeed, given the general lack of toleration for debate in the current United States Air Force, it is astonishing that he is still regarded as a hero.

A number of factors drove the development of US air power during the interwar period. Part of the explanation has to do with the fact that the great distances in North America made the speed associated with flight more economically attractive to Americans. Consequently, there was more interest than in Europe in providing governmental subsidies to air passenger and mail services. And the distances that aircraft had to cover in the United States encouraged both airframe and engine development – a factor that would contribute to the development of first-rate military prototypes by the late 1930s.

The United States Congress also played a role in pushing air power within the army and navy. In the case of the latter, the congressional mandate that only qualified aviators could command aircraft carriers and aviation units encouraged a number of senior officers to qualify. The future admiral William Halsey qualified so late in life (he was already a grandfather) that no one *ever* trusted him to land or take off an aircraft by himself. Such encouragement made the navy's senior leadership more air-minded than was the case in the Royal Navy. Their understanding helped to push the edge of technology to the point where, by early 1943, US carriers possessed fighter aircraft every bit as good as their land-based equivalents, which was not the case with the aircraft on the Royal Navy's carriers.

Thinking about the implications of aircraft carrier and air power began well before the United States even owned a carrier. By his own choice Admiral William Sims returned to the Naval War College after commanding US naval forces in Europe during the First World War. There he instituted a series of war games testing the utilization of aircraft from carriers, beyond that of simply spotting the fall of shells for the battle fleet. Equally important for the development of naval aviation in the early 1920s was the appointment of William Moffett to head a new bureau, the Bureau of Aeronautics, a powerful position from which he guided much of the thrust of naval air power. Through political connections Moffett remained as the head of BuAer until his death in the early 1930s in the crash of the airship *Akron*.

The US Navy enjoyed another advantage over the Royal Navy. The Washington Naval Treaty of 1922 confronted the Americans, as with the British and Japanese, with the problem of what to do with the half-finished hulls of the battle-cruisers *Lexington* and *Saratoga*. The completion of the two ships provided the US Navy with large fast

The largest and most luxurious flying boat of its era was the giant Boeing 314 Clipper which flew Pan American Airways first commercial trans-Atlantic services in June 1939. A fleet of nine Boeing 314s flew throughout the Second World War with Pan American and BOAC carrying thousands of VIPs and priority military passengers and cargo without loss.

carriers, a major advantage in experimenting with the tactical employment of naval air power. By the late 1930s the US Navy, still in control of its naval air assets, was utilizing numbers of aircraft on the deck parks of their carriers that were inconceivable from the Royal Navy's point of view.

In the 1920s naval aviators used Mitchell's strident attacks on the navy to gain leverage with the more hidebound admirals. Nevertheless, as a whole the US Navy's leadership proved supportive in developing the potential of carrier aviation. The relationship between the Naval War College – in evaluating and designing war games and fleet exercises – the fleet and the fleet exercises themselves were particularly fruitful. Ironically, one of those exercises in the 1930s featured a carrier attack on an opposing fleet in Pearl Harbor. The result of such innovations was that naval aviators worked out many of the problems associated with integrating aircraft into fleet operations. The result of such innovations showed clearly in the devastating carrier offensive the Americans waged in the Pacific from 1943.

The separate path taken by naval air power exercised an important and beneficial influence on engine development in the United States. In a theoretical sense, in-line engines offered greater potential than radial engines. But it was easier to solve the problems involved in developing more powerful radial engines than was the case with in-line engines. Moreover, radial engines were considerably easier to maintain, since all mechanics had to do to get at the working parts was remove the cowling. It was this latter advantage that pushed the US Navy to choose radial engines over in-line engines for carrier aircraft, for even on the large carriers like the *Lexington* and *Saratoga* it was difficult to work on aircraft in heavy seas. By the early 1930s radial engines developed for naval aircraft were offering considerable advantages in ease of maintenance and reliability over in-line engines. As a result, US aircraft manufacturers turned to radial engines for aeroplanes like the DC-2 and DC-3. These naval developments also influenced the Army Air Corps and its engine and aircraft procurement programmes. The radial engine allowed Boeing to produce the B-17, the first true American strategic bomber, in 1936.

The development of radial engines eventually provided naval and land-based American air forces, with aircraft that were every bit as good as anything possessed by European air forces, but considerably easier to maintain. Beside superior naval aircraft like the Hellcat and Corsair, radial engines powered P-47s, B-17s, B-24s, B-25s, B-26s, and C-47s, among others. Without the push from naval aviation, it is likely that the Army Air Corps would have throttled development of radial engines in favour of in-line engines as the RAF did – to the detriment not only of naval aviation, but of its own future capabilities as well.

Mitchell's court martial has led air-power advocates to argue that the army suppressed the advancement of air power in the interwar period. Nothing could be further from the truth. With substantial support from many in Congress, the Army Air Corps took the view that air power would represent *the* dominant feature of future conflicts. By the early 1930s the Air Corps Tactical School, the main army school for Air Corps officers, had moved away from Mitchell's opinion that the enemy's air force should be the main target. Now the belief was not only that bombers would be the crucial factor, but that they would face little serious opposition in the next war.

Thus, American airmen developed a complex doctrine and concept of air power every bit as dogmatic as the RAF's beliefs, but with substantial differences. Like the British, the Americans argued that bombers could fight their way through enemy defences. By the mid 1930s American aircraft manufacturers, particularly Boeing, were producing bombers with greater range, load-carrying capacity, speed and survivability. With its defending machine-guns, the B-17 appeared to epitomize the potential for large bomber formations to fight their way through enemy airspace. Moreover, the invention of the Norden bombsight (developed by the navy) had seemingly solved the problem of hitting targets accurately.

As for bomber targets, American air pundits argued for attacks on the enemy's economic structure rather than on cities and morale. This partly resulted from political realities. Arguments for attacks on population centres would have been damaging under the political circumstances prevailing in the United States. American theorists therefore argued that all economic systems possessed nodal targets, the destruction of which would lead to wide-ranging effects on the economic system as a whole. Such targets might include transportation, refineries, ball-bearing production and electrical power networks. Like the British, the Americans believed that once the enemy was under aerial attack, the population, under the strain of economic dislocation, would be unable to stand the pressure of sustained bombing.

The result of such doctrinal beliefs presented the US Army Air Force with considerable difficulty in adapting to the actual conditions of war. American doctrine excluded the possibility of long-range escorts for bombers, not so much because they were not technologically feasible, but because they were not needed. Ironically, by the early 1930s the navy already possessed prototypes of fighter aircraft with substantial range and other advantages over those that the Army Air Corps possessed. But, then as now, there existed a 'not-invented here' syndrome.

Moreover, tests of the Norden bombsight and precision bombing occurred in unrealistic circumstances: on bombing ranges in the south-western United States, in conditions of perfect visibility, with bombers dropping on an individual basis and with no hostile anti-aircraft or enemy fighters. Not surprisingly, when compared to actual results under combat conditions, Air Corps estimates of bombing potential proved wildly optimistic. That should not be surprising; what was inexcusable was the persistence with which US Army Air Force leaders, particularly in the Eighth Air Force in the summer and autumn of 1943, conducted operations in accordance with doctrinal precepts despite the evidence from actual combat.

The greatest advantage the Americans enjoyed in developing the aircraft's potential as a weapon lay in their immense industrial base.

That economic strength provided for the mass production of four-engined bombers as well as the resources to develop some of the war's most outstanding aircraft. Given the dominance of economics in America's *Weltanschauung*, its airmen were particularly attracted to the idea of attacking the enemy's industrial base. But as an advocate of that theory admitted after the war,

> by accepting a concept based upon nonaccumulation of risks or problems, [American airmen] admitted [their] inability to recognize that in the realm of force application, a single factor or condition cannot be changed without affecting the other factors. [They] ignored what seemingly was obvious: that each premise, supported assumptions, contained inherent weaknesses. Taken individually, the shortcomings were not serious; if taken collectively, they might have undermined the entire concept.

In fact, as we shall see, their assumptions came perilously close to doing just that.

THE GERMANS

A number of historians have argued that military institutions always focus on the last war and that is why they do badly in the next. In fact, that view is largely wrong. The Germans were the only European military power to study the lessons of the First World War in detail and then build their theory, training and preparations for the next conflict in accordance with what had actually happened in the last. In 1920 the new chief of the general staff, Hans von Seeckt, ordered the establishment of no less than fifty-seven committees to examine the tactical and operational lessons of the First World War. Among those committees were a number that examined what had happened in the air. Their efforts resulted in a series of reports that contributed significantly to German thinking about air war throughout the interwar period.

But no matter how realistically the Germans viewed the future in the 1920s, they were confronted by the fact that the Treaty of Versailles prevented them from possessing military and multi-engine aircraft. After 1926, the Allies allowed the Germans to build the latter type of aircraft for civil aviation. The resulting national airline, Lufthansa, provided a modicum of technological and flying experience on which a future air force might draw. But even here there were problems; most civil aviation in Europe involved relatively short distances and thus the development of engines and airframes was more limited than it was in the United States. This factor would put the Germans at a disadvantage in developing sufficiently powerful engines for a four-engined bomber in the late 1930s and early 1940s.

In order to gain experience, the Germans did co-operate extensively with the Soviets on bases located deep in Russia. Here German fliers received training on military aircraft, but the Soviets probably gained

When the pride of the German airship fleet, Hindenburg, *burst into flames as it docked at the US Naval Air Station at Lakehurst on the evening of 6 June 1937, after crossing the Atlantic, it sounded the death knell for commercial airship operations. Thirteen passengers and twenty-three crew were killed.*

more in knowledge of engineering and production techniques than did the Germans. However, such theorizing and secretive effort changed with Adolf Hitler's appointment as Chancellor in late January 1933. The new Nazi regime immediately embarked on massive rearmament; among many objectives was the creation of a powerful independent air force. The head of the new Luftwaffe was an energetic First World War ace, Hermann Goering, who had won a reputation as the Führer's ruthless and devoted follower. Goering would remain inextricably linked with the Luftwaffe's fate almost to the end in spring 1945.

For much of the Third Reich's first years Goering remained only a titular commander of the Luftwaffe, as he was involved in helping Hitler and the Nazi Party subvert the state and consolidate their hold on power. However, Goering possessed a number of competent subordinates transferred from the army. Some, such as Hans Jeschonnek, who graduated first in his class from the *Kriegsakademie*, had served as pilots in the First World War; others, like Albert Kesselring or Walther Wever, had had no air experience in the war and learned to fly in the Luftwaffe. That the army thought particularly highly of the new service's chief of staff, Wever, is suggested by the fact that the other candidate for the job was the future field marshal, Erich von Manstein.

The new service confronted daunting problems. It had to build a combat force out of very little, in a strategic atmosphere which, as Hitler indicated, might soon involve the Reich in war. Germany had a small industrial base of squabbling aircraft firms on which to begin the build-up; in 1933 the aircraft industry possessed only 4,000 workers; by fall 1938 that number had swelled to over 204,000. Despite the army's interest in aviation, few army officers possessed real experience, and even most of that was dated. Still, Goering picked two exceptional individuals to conduct the build-up. The Luftwaffe's chief of staff, Wever, had participated in the development of the German army's doctrine in 1917 and 1918, a process that had revolutionized the ground war in 1918. The second key individual was Erhard Milch, who had considerable First World War experience and who played a major role

Built to fly sixty-six passengers non-stop across the Atlantic, the twelve-engined 157-foot wingspan Dornier Do X only managed one trans-Atlantic flight in 1931 – which took almost nine months to complete with only its ten-man crew aboard.

in Lufthansa's growth into the dominant civil airline in central Europe. Both men possessed formidable organizational talents: Wever set the course for the creation of an effective combat force as well as developing an intelligent and coherent air doctrine; Milch brought his skills to bear on the expansion of production and the Luftwaffe's logistical structure.

The Luftwaffe was certainly not 'the handmaiden of the army' as many post-war air-power historians claimed. Its leaders recognized air power as an equal factor with the traditional services in the conduct of war. While air-power theorists in the United States and Britain almost exclusively emphasized strategic bombing, the Luftwaffe's leaders recognized that air power involved a wide range of functions, many of which were as important as strategic bombing. To begin with, the Germans believed that the political, strategic and geographic context within which war took place would determine how best to use air power. The Germans also argued that gaining air superiority was crucial to the waging of any air campaign. Not surprisingly, given the Reich's geographic position, support for the army, particularly in terms of strikes against an enemy's transportation system, was central to the German view of air war. In the late 1930s the Germans were more dubious about the value of close air support, an opinion undoubtedly driven by the heavy losses their ground attack aircraft had suffered in 1918.

But the Luftwaffe did not ignore strategic bombing. Until his death in 1936 Wever argued that strategic bombing might be of considerable utility in a future war, but only over a long period. Others in the Luftwaffe were more enthusiastic; one argument in some Luftwaffe circles was that with the new *Volksgemeinschaft* (racial community), Nazi Germany would be able to endure enemy air attacks better than any democratic or communist state. This was not a dominant attitude, but it was popular among some like Albert Kesselring, and it was certainly attractive to Nazi leaders like Goering and Hitler.

From 1933 to 1939 the Luftwaffe underwent a massive expansion as well as complete replacement with a new generation of aircraft. By 1937 the Germans had the Bf 109 and He 111 in production, while production of the Ju 88 began in 1939. These aircraft dominated the Luftwaffe's force structure through to 1944; the transition itself proved difficult and costly, as it did for other air forces in the world. The new generation of stressed-skin monoplanes with more powerful engines were not only more difficult to fly and land, but more complicated and difficult to maintain. The fact that the Luftwaffe was also in the middle of a massive expansion programme exacerbated its problems in adjusting to the new generation of aircraft. Flying squadrons ran high accident rates, particularly in Bf 109 squadrons, where that aircraft's narrow undercarriage proved a killer for inexperienced pilots. One pilot watched his squadron wreck four aircraft and kill two pilots in an afternoon's work in summer 1938. Bomber and fighter squadrons ran in-commission rates of barely 50 per cent throughout the period – making laughable the claims of historians that the Luftwaffe could have attacked the British Isles, if the Czech crisis had exploded into war.

The Germans were more realistic about aircrew and aircraft capabilities than their counterparts in the United States and Britain.

They addressed the technological possibilities quite differently. From their experiences in the First World War, reaffirmed by their experience in Spain, the Germans recognized that bombing accuracy at night or during periods of bad weather was going to be difficult. Thus, by 1939 the Luftwaffe had begun equipping its aircraft with blind-bombing and bad-weather devices; the RAF had no such technology until 1942, while the Americans would have to borrow from the RAF in 1943 and 1944 to support their efforts during bad weather. Moreover, the Germans put considerable effort into developing a long-range escort fighter, the Bf 110; that aircraft proved incapable of handling the lighter single-seat interceptor planes, but at least the Germans attempted to address the problem of supporting bombers with fighter escorts.

Throughout the late 1930s and into the 1940s the Germans mounted a major effort to develop a long-range strategic bomber to replace the twin-engined aircraft with which the Luftwaffe had initially equipped its bomber squadrons. The first aircraft in this developmental process was the Ju 88, the so-called '*Schnell*' (fast) bomber; the initial concept was quite similar to what the De Havilland would turn into the Mosquito, arguably the most effective strategic bomber of the war. The first Ju 88 prototype weighed 7 tons and had a top speed of 350 miles per hour. But the Luftwaffe design bureau introduced 250,000 design changes, increasing the aircraft's weight to 12 tons and reducing its speed to 250 miles per hour. Still the Ju 88 proved one of the finest multi-role aircraft in the Second World War. But it might have achieved even more had Luftwaffe and Junkers engineers not made such drastic changes.

The attempt to develop a four-engined, long-range bomber turned into the Luftwaffe's greatest failure. In 1936 the Air Ministry had cancelled two four-engined bomber development programmes. It did so, not because the leadership had lost interest in a strategic bomber, but rather because it had two sitting ducks on its hands, whose speeds and load capacities were completely inadequate. Long-range bomber development was one area where the Germans remained at a disadvantage as a result of the Treaty of Versailles. Without military aircraft, the Germans had not been able to work on engine problems associated with long-range flight, while German civil aviation had focused on aircraft of relatively short range – suitable for flights between the cities of central and western Europe rather than the considerably longer distances of the British Empire or the United States.

Nevertheless, the Germans ploughed ahead. Their solution to the power plant problem was ingenious, but technologically unfeasible: they designed the ill-fated He 177 with two nacelles, and with two engines welded together in each nacelle, thus providing the necessary power while cutting down on drag. The British attempted a similar design in the early 1940s with their Manchester bomber. But given the state of technology the design was not feasible. The He 177 engines had a tendency to decouple violently in flight, the resulting mixture of broken fuel lines, spewing oil, high heat and electrical sparks usually bringing flights to a spectacular conclusion. The British had the sense to stop the Manchester experiment and redesign the aircraft with four nacelles as well as give it a new name, the Lancaster. But the Germans, with inordinate arrogance, persisted with the two-nacelle design through to 1944 – a five-year period. There was another peculiarity the He 177 possessed that indicates that maintenance was not a high priority with its designers: the entire two-engine assembly had to be removed just to replace the spark plugs.

The Luftwaffe exercised an increasingly baleful influence over European politics as the 1930s drew to a close. In March 1935 Hitler declared the obvious: that German rearmament was in full swing and that it included an independent air force. In 1936 the Germans sent a small force of 'volunteers', the so-called 'Condor Legion', to Spain to aid General Francisco Franco in his attempt to overthrow the Spanish republic. Unlike Mussolini, Hitler had little interest in seeing Franco gain a quick victory. Rather, the war served to distract Europe's Left from the real danger: German rearmament. Thus, the Germans sent only small ground and air forces to the Iberian peninsula, compared to the large Italian expeditionary force.

Nevertheless, Spain proved a wonderful test bed for Luftwaffe aircraft and technology as well as for its ideas about air power. Barely 200 German aircraft participated in the war, but that was enough to show that current Luftwaffe aircraft were not up to the mark; the weaknesses of the Ju 52 as a bomber and He 51 as a fighter pushed the Luftwaffe's senior leadership into introducing the next generation of aircraft more quickly, particularly the Bf 109 and the He 111. Experience in Spain also helped develop the finger-four, in which a four aircraft flight took up the positions of four extended fingers. That tactical approach provided the Luftwaffe with a considerable advantage in its first combat with British fighters. On the other hand, the Germans remained too optimistic about the effectiveness of 88 mm anti-aircraft guns against aircraft, although they did discover the utility of that weapon against enemy tanks.

The Spanish Civil War was also of use in allowing the Germans to redevelop the close air-support tactics they had used in March 1918. However, their tactical conceptions largely focused on the breakthrough battle and remained primitive in nature. For example, the

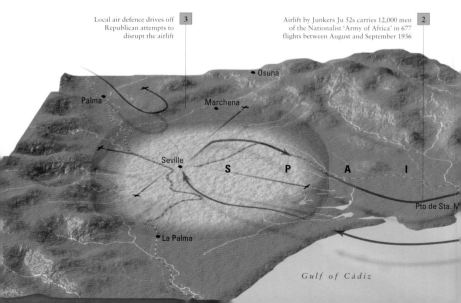

Local air defence drives off Republican attempts to disrupt the airlift **3**

Airlift by Junkers Ju 52s carries 12,000 men of the Nationalist 'Army of Africa' in 677 flights between August and September 1936 **2**

Osuna

Palma

Marchena

Seville

S P A I

Pto de Sta. M

La Palma

Gulf of Cádiz

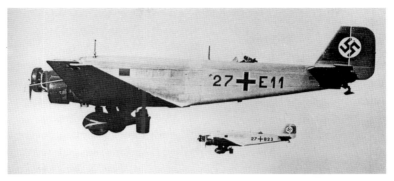

Developed originally as a civil airliner, Luftwaffe Junkers Ju 52s were used in the Spanish Civil War as bombers and transports; they proved crucial in airlifting Franco's troops from North Africa to the Spanish Civil War battlefields during the summer of 1936.

Air War over Spain

With the help of Adolf Hitler, Nationalist General Franco was able to airlift his troops from North Africa on Ju 52s of the German Condor Legion to gain a crucial stronghold in Southern Spain in the early days of the Spanish Civil War.

Republican naval units control the sea around the Spanish coast **1**

Mediterranean Sea

Gibraltar

Ceuta • Tetuan

Strait of Gibraltar

MOROCCO (Spanish)

• Tangier

ádiz

ATLANTIC OCEAN

first use of close air support with infantry involved the infantry sewing large white circles on their backs – one suspects not only for identification purposes by friendly aircraft, but also to discourage them from retreating. Ironically, in terms of the myth of the tank–Stuka team (a mirage of the Goebbels propaganda machine), the Luftwaffe developed no capability in the late 1930s to provide support to armoured and mechanized forces in a mobile war. Throughout the Polish and French campaigns, the Luftwaffe inadvertently bombed German mechanized spearheads, although one army unit reported that in general the Luftwaffe hit the Poles more often than their own troops. Not until April 1940 did the Luftwaffe and army first experiment with forward observers with spearhead units. Nevertheless, the Germans were at least working on the problem; the British would not employ a similar system until 1942, and the Americans in 1943.

In 1938 the Luftwaffe's re-equipping and expansion was in full swing. Consequently, maintenance difficulties, the training of new crews and supply problems beset operating units and rendered it a military instrument incapable of sustained air operations. Thus, even a limited effort to support an attack on Czechoslovakia would have strained the Luftwaffe to breaking-point. Moreover, as war-games in August 1938 indicated, the Luftwaffe had no chance of executing a sustained strategic bombing campaign against Britain. Any such attempt would only have resulted in dropping bombs haphazardly over the British landscape. Ironically the Luftwaffe achieved its greatest success by persuading British and particularly French military and political leaders that their countries were about to come under a rain of bombs. In the end, the Munich sacrifice of Czechoslovakia was to a great extent the result of unjustified fears about German air superiority.

By 1939 the Luftwaffe's combat capabilities had improved dramatically; its impact on Europe's diplomacy was less dramatic, however. Re-equipment of its air squadrons was well in hand, and the Ju 88 was about to come into production. Moreover, the strategic situation had changed radically in the Reich's favour, especially with the signing of the Nazi–Soviet Non-Aggression Pact. The Luftwaffe was now the world's most advanced air force, capable of dealing effective blows against its enemies. Not only was it equipped to win air superiority over a rapidly moving battlefield, but it could also render significant support to the army in their efforts to break through enemy front lines. This broad-based approach allowed the Luftwaffe to play a crucial role in the German victories in the early years of the Second World War. With a wide selection of capabilities, it significantly enhanced the army's conduct of ground operations while preventing enemy air forces from interfering with the advance of German ground forces.

However, by the late 1930s Luftwaffe attitudes and thinking were already suffering from the insidious influence of Nazi ideology. Wever's death undoubtedly accelerated the process, while Goering's rapid promotion of officers thoroughly imbued with Nazi ideology also contributed. This led not only to a substantial underestimation of Germany's potential opponents, particularly Britain and the Soviet Union (as well as the United States), but also their minimizing the connection between ends and means. Shortly after Munich, Hitler demanded a five-fold expansion of the Luftwaffe, an expansion that would have cost a sum equivalent to that which had been spent on German rearmament between 1933 and 1939 as a whole, and would have required 85 per cent of the world's supply of aviation gasoline. When senior officers pointed this out to Hans Jeschonnek, soon to become the Luftwaffe's chief of staff, he replied, 'Gentlemen, in my view, it is our duty to support the Führer and not to work against him.' On such blind faith in Hitler and in the inherent racial superiority of the German *Volk* the Luftwaffe would founder in the coming war.

THE OTHER AIR FORCES

It is impossible to cover the other air forces of the world in detail. Nevertheless, there are significant points to be made about developments in other major powers: in particular in Italy, France, the Soviet Union and Japan. The Italians, of course, produced the most famous theorist of air power, Giulio Douhet. Douhet had been at the forefront of Italian efforts in the First World War to find a means of driving the Austro-Hungarian army out of its impregnable positions in the foothills of the Alps. In fact, the technological means were not yet available, and would not be available until the early years of the Second World War, for conducting a truly effective strategic bombing campaign. The casualty bill that Italy had suffered in the First World War, well over 500,000 dead, did nothing to lessen Douhet's enthusiasm for air power. Nor did it make Mussolini's regime any less keen on trumpeting Douhet's theories as a means of realizing its vision of Italy as an emerging great power, one that would regain Rome's Mediterranean empire.

Ironically, no nation in Europe was less well-positioned to establish such capabilities. Italy had neither the technological nor the industrial base to build an air force that could dominate Europe. Moreover, Italy was more vulnerable to enemy air attacks, since its industry was located close to its northern borders, than were its potential opponents. Nevertheless, the size of the Italian military budget should certainly have prepared the *Regia Aeronautica* for a major role in the coming war. In fact, Italian defence expenditures from 1933 to 1938 were greater than those of either France or Britain.

But the Fascist regime got precious little return for its expenditure on Italy's military, largely because the megalomaniacal strategic policy resulted in a series of ill-advised foreign adventures. In September 1935 the Italians invaded Abyssinia, and by the following spring, had conquered it. That conquest added worthless and strategically indefensible territory to the Italian empire, at great cost. In the beginning the Italians came close to losing, but the massive use of poison gas dispensed from Italian aircraft against defenceless Abyssinian levies led to victory.

Almost immediately after the Abyssinian adventure, civil war broke out in Spain, and Mussolini committed sizeable Italian ground and air forces to the support of Franco's nationalists. The war in Spain dragged on for three dreadful years of bloodletting; it also proved a terrible

The Italian Savoia-Marchetti S.M.81 Pipistrello *first flew in 1935 and, although it was obsolete by 1940, it was used as a night bomber until 1942. This example belonged to the 202a* Squadriglia, *40th* Gruppo, *38th* Stormo, *operating over Albania in 1941.*

drain on the Italian exchequer and its military forces. There were serious consequences for all three Italian military services, but particularly for the air force, the most serious being that it froze aircraft development. It was not that the Italians were incapable of developing first-rate aircraft – by 1942 they had proved that they were – but in the late 1930s the resources were not available for developing the kinds of aircraft which other European air forces were acquiring. As a result, the Italians went to war with an air force that was more out of date than the French air force – the French were at least bringing into service a new generation of aircraft.

The French case is particularly tragic because they did not miss by much. With an independent air force, they confronted the same set of technological, production and organizational issues that beset the other major air forces in the mid 1930s. Historians have often described the French air force's industrial base as outdated and obsolete; but the German aircraft industry was in even worse shape in January 1933, when the Nazis came to power. Admittedly, the French were producing obsolete fighters and bombers in 1933, but then the Ju 52 was hardly on the leading edge of technology. While the French air force possessed a large number of obsolete aircraft, it at least possessed a large number of experienced pilots.

Unfortunately for the French, the next generation of aircraft demanded major investments in design, plant and production facilities. But political circumstances delayed revitalization of the productive base until too late. Unlike the British, the French recognized the growing danger on the other side of the Rhine. But there were political impediments to a substantial upswing in military spending. On one hand, the army maintained a solid control over defence policy and throttled debate in regards to air matters. Until 1937 its leadership remained *blasé* about the German air threat; then army leaders panicked and contributed to the collapse of French will in the late 1930s.

But more important to French unpreparedness in the air was the triumph of the Popular Front in 1936 under the socialist Léon Blum. However controversial Blum's social legislation, what really damaged air force prospects was the government's refusal to increase expenditure on the aircraft industry's base, research and development, and production. The result was that, while the Luftwaffe progressed to a new generation of aircraft in 1937–8 and the RAF in 1938–9, the French did not begin the transition period until late 1939. Thus, while they were bringing on line first-rate aircraft in 1940, French air squadrons ran into similar problems of maintenance, accidents, inexperienced air crews and low operational-readiness rates that had plagued the Luftwaffe and RAF in the preceding years. But the French experienced these problems just as the great battles in the Low Countries erupted.

To the east, the Soviets showed considerable interest in air power; after all it was a clear attribute of modernization. But as is typical in Russian history, their technological base lagged behind that of the industrialized West. Co-operation with the German military, which continued through the last years of the Weimar Republic, undoubtedly helped the Soviets more than the Germans, but there were limits to what the Soviets could draw from their German partners. By the mid 1930s, the Soviets were clearly on the way to developing the base for air power, with the factories and engineers on which war in the twentieth century rested. There were, of course, weaknesses, particularly with training and the tactical preparation of flying formations, but by 1937 they had developed the engineering expertise to design simple, rugged, easy-to-maintain aircraft which were effective in operation.

Unfortunately for the Soviet air force and its sister services, Stalin's purge of the military began in May 1937. The results were catastrophic. The Soviet Union's secret police devastated the air force's officer corps and caused a paralysis that delayed the transition to a new generation of aircraft until 1941. Thus, when the Wehrmacht struck, the Soviets found themselves in the same position that the French had been the year before – with an air force that was technologically inferior. Moreover, those units that were changing to new aircraft possessed neither the training nor maintenance to support the new fighters and bombers. The combination of obsolete aircraft, ill-trained pilots and a late transition to the next generation of aircraft would prove even more deadly for the Soviet air force than for the French air force the year before.

The Japanese developed their army and naval air forces in the seeming isolation of Asia. But they paid close attention to what was occurring throughout the rest of the world. In the early stages of development they received considerable help from the Royal Navy in the development of their naval air force. In the early 1920s the Japanese made slow progress; even more than the British and American navies, the Imperial Japanese Navy was in the grasp of the gun club of battleship admirals. But like the Americans, the Japanese benefited from the Washington Naval Treaty of 1922; they converted the hulls of one battle cruiser and one battleship then under construction into aircraft carriers. In 1922 the Japanese created an independent naval air headquarters which provided a directing centre and focus for naval aviation. Moreover, in the late 1920s the Japanese received an infusion of radial engine technology from the United States.

The increasing control of the Japanese government by right-wing militarists in the early 1930s led to the seizure of Manchuria in 1931. Then, in 1937 the Japanese military launched a massive invasion of China. The support the military received for these adventures, as well as the perception in the Japanese military that a war was coming to the United States, led to substantial and innovative aircraft designs. The Japanese learned a great deal from their wars in Asia. Because of their isolated geographic position in Asia, they had no interest in strategic bombing. It was inconceivable that Japan itself would ever be in the position to attack London, Moscow or Washington directly. But the Russo-Japanese War of 1904–5 suggested the possibility of dealing the Soviet Union, Britain or the United States such devastating defeats in the Pacific theatre that Japan could have its own way there.

Japan's future opponents, the US Navy and the Royal Navy made the terrible mistake of underestimating not only Japanese tactical proficiency, but also the technological level Japan had achieved by the early 1940s. By then the Japanese were no longer in the business of copying European technology; the weapons they were now making were equal or superior. The Zero, which entered service in the Japanese navy in the late 1930s, was in many respects the equal of the Spitfire and the Bf 109, and was certainly far superior to anything possessed by the British and the Americans in the Pacific, when the war began in that theatre. Moreover, the Zero possessed a range superior to that of any other fighter of the early 1940s. However, the Japanese achieved these capabilities at a price. The Zero had neither self-sealing tanks nor armour protection for its pilots, which made it extraordinarily light, but also vulnerable.

Japanese naval pilots went through the toughest training programme anywhere in the world. The future ace, Saburo Sakai, describes himself and his fellow pilots as attempting to snatch flies out of the air and spot stars in full daylight. Having gained considerable combat experience in the 'China Incident', their murderous invasion of China which had involved only light casualties, the Japanese went to war in 1941 with an extraordinarily well-trained pilot force. Yet without armour and self-sealing tanks their pilots would suffer high casualties no matter what the combat capabilities of their aircraft. Moreover, there would be few replacements, because the Japanese high command refused to make changes to the rigorous syllabuses of their flying schools, despite the fact that over 90 per cent of the trainees dropped out. Thus if the war continued and Japanese losses mounted, there would not be adequate replacements for those lost.

Like the Germans, the Japanese counted on will and the warrior spirit to overcome whatever difficulties they confronted. Calculations of means and ends were simply not part of their strategic or operational equations. The result was that while the Japanese air forces might gain stunning successes at the beginning of any war, the inexorable laws of losses in air war would eventually work against them.

CONCLUSION

The interwar period represented an extraordinary leap forward in the technology of war. When the First World War ended in November 1918, men had been flying for less than twenty years. In the 1920s there was much theorizing about the future of air power. However, both the intellectual climate and the exhaustion of victors and vanquished alike resulted in low levels of expenditures on defence. In such circumstances there were relatively few technological advances. But during this period airmen laid the groundwork for the explosion of technological developments in the 1930s. The growing international crisis in the 1930s resulted in the untying of purse strings; the dictatorships began a great armaments race, but within a relatively short period the democracies were in the race too.

The resulting technological revolution saw the replacement of the biplane technology of the First World War with the introduction of all-metal, monoplane designs that doubled the speed of the aircraft. Along with the explosion of aircraft technology came a host of technological supports for war in the air: radar, blind-bombing devices, bad-weather-navigation and landing devices, radio control and others. But how these advances would work out in the conduct of actual air campaigns and battles no one could say until the bombs began to drop and the lights again went out in Europe.

CHAPTER THREE

The Air War
in Europe

*Heinkel He 111 bombers in formation on their
way to targets in Britain in the summer of
1940. The Luftwaffe lacked a significant force
of long-range bombers and it remained an
essentially tactical arm throughout the War.*

The Air War in Europe

THEORISTS OF AIR POWER during the interwar period had posited that strategic bombing would be the essential element in a future European war. In so far as strategic bombing's contribution to the eventual victory of Allied forces in the war is concerned, they were right. But with regard to virtually everything else in respect to air power they were wrong. Air power's greatest contribution to the Allied triumph lay in its versatility; it was in the very breadth of its contribution that the aeroplane made its mark in the Second World War. In the air defence of Great Britain, in the long dreary flights over the Atlantic in search of U-boats, in support of ground operations, in airborne operations, in its role as a reconnaissance vehicle, aircraft contributed immeasurably to victory over the Third Reich.

But even in their estimates of what strategic bombing might achieve, the theorists were wrong about a great deal. Strategic bombing proved to be more of a sledge hammer than a rapier. It was the weight of the Allied bombing, a weight of bombing that turned much of Germany to dust, that finally broke the Nazi war economy. Moreover, that effort proved immensely costly in terms of the lives of the aircrew as well as their aircraft. Ironically, strategic bombing replicated the attrition of the Western Front in the First World War, except that this time the losses fell largely on 'the best and the brightest'. In the end though, strategic bombing worked its effects because of the concomitant pressures that ground and naval war exercised on the Third Reich. Moreover, many of its most important effects, such as the achievement of air superiority over the European continent, the diversion of a considerable portion of Germany's heavy artillery to air defence, and the vast misappropriation of resources to the V-2 rocket programme were unintended and unforeseen consequences of the bomber offensive.

It took four years (1939–43) for the Allies to develop the broad spectrum of capabilities that made air power so deadly to their enemies. Unfortunately, when the war began in 1939, the Germans possessed the only military that had proved willing to address air power in its widest applications, rather than in the narrow conception that strategic bombing offered the only proper employment for air power. Thus, with a clearer understanding of air power's real potential as well as a ferociously effective approach to war on the ground, the Germans came close to destroying European civilization.

THE EARLY CAMPAIGNS OF THE SECOND WORLD WAR

In the war that began on 1 September 1939 air power played a crucial role from the start. The Germans considered a massive opening attack on Warsaw, but bad weather forced them to attack alternative targets. The Luftwaffe's most important contribution in the Polish campaign lay in quickly gaining air superiority; the Poles were skilled opponents, but they possessed obsolete aircraft which were no match for those of the Germans. Luftwaffe bombers struck particularly at cities and transportation links, which thoroughly disrupted the Polish mobilization.

The Junkers Ju 87 Stuka dive-bomber was slow, lightly armed, and vulnerable when it met fighter opposition. However, the Stuka was none the less a devastating weapon in the Polish and French Blitzkrieg campaigns bringing death, accompanied by a screaming siren, from the unopposed skies .

A small number of Luftwaffe aircraft directly supported the drive of the German panzer forces which completely broke the Polish army apart in the first week of the campaign. Close air-support strikes were mostly successful; however, one Wehrmacht battalion, bombed for several hours by the Luftwaffe, suggested that courts martial might be in order.

After Poland, the Germans carefully analyzed their success and planned the coming air and ground campaigns against the West with those lessons in mind. The first strike came against Denmark and Norway; without the Luftwaffe's contribution the attack on Norway would have been impossible. Inexcusably, the Norwegians were caught by surprise except in the Oslo fiord, where the protecting forts, manned by reservists, wrecked the German heavy cruiser, the *Blücher*, and threatened to thwart the Nazi attempt to seize the capital. However, early the following morning Luftwaffe paratroopers captured Oslo's airport and throughout the day reinforcements were flown in by Ju 52 transports. By early afternoon the invaders were strong enough to move on the capital. At Kristiansand paratroopers seized the airfield, and the Luftwaffe flew in reinforcements as well as bomber and fighter aircraft. With the airfields in its hands, the Luftwaffe gained air superiority over southern and central Norway; consequently, German air power could intervene effectively in the land battle against the disorganized Norwegians, as well as dominating the seas off Norway. The Royal Navy quickly discovered the vulnerability of its ships against aircraft; pre-war arguments that ships could survive in areas where enemy air power was present had been proved wrong, but sadly the lesson was not completely absorbed in the Royal Navy.

As the Norwegian campaign moved towards its close, the Wehrmacht struck against the Low Countries and France. On 10 May 'Case Yellow' – the code name for the western offensive – kicked off with a massive assault on Allied airfields. However, the Allied air forces were ready, and the Germans did little significant damage. Over the course of a day of furious dogfights and attacks on airfields, transportation centres and other military targets, the Luftwaffe

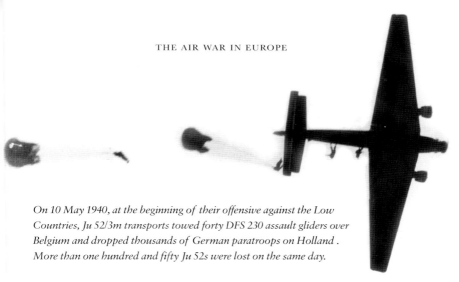

On 10 May 1940, at the beginning of their offensive against the Low Countries, Ju 52/3m transports towed forty DFS 230 assault gliders over Belgium and dropped thousands of German paratroops on Holland . More than one hundred and fifty Ju 52s were lost on the same day.

suffered fearful losses – no less than eighty-three aircraft, more than on any other day in 1940, including the Battle of Britain.

The Luftwaffe's largest success on the first day was not in the air battle, but in its support for the ground forces. Luftwaffe paratroopers seized the bridges leading into Fortress Holland and held them until the 9th Panzer Division could destroy the defences completely. But German paratroopers failed to seize the Hague by a *coup de main*, as the Dutch defenders drove the attackers off the capital's airfield. Nevertheless, the boldness of the airborne landings distracted the Dutch from the main German drive. On 15 May the Dutch surrendered, their decision helped by the terror-bombing of Rotterdam by the Luftwaffe – an attack that in the best traditions of Douhet and strategic-bombing advocates killed over 800 civilians and rendered 80,000 homeless. At that time the Germans were not reluctant to talk enthusiastically about the impact of their bombing on Dutch morale.

In Belgium less than two hundred glider-borne troops landed on the top of the great fortress at Eben Emael and quickly blinded the defenders by destroying their viewing ports – a stunning coup that opened the way for General Fedor von Bock's push into central Belgium, where the Allies expected the main German effort to come. In central Belgium, the Luftwaffe did nothing to hinder the main Allied

A Messerschmitt Bf 109E-3 of JG 2 'Richthofen' with its ground crew in France 1940, waiting for orders to attack England. Fitted with two 7.9mm MG 17 fuselage guns and two wing-mounted 20mm MG FF cannon, the Bf 109E Emil helped to destroy the air forces of Europe in the early campaigns of the war.

push, since Allied troops were rushing into a trap. The main German advance came through the Ardennes. Here the Luftwaffe put up a vast umbrella over panzer forces sweeping through the Ardennes. Nevertheless, Allied air attacks did disturb the Germans. Obsolete British 'Battle' light bombers suffered terrible losses on 10 May: of thirty-two committed, thirteen were shot down, while the rest limped home damaged. Yet on 12 May General Heinz Guderian's panzer corps was screaming about heavy Allied bombing attacks over the Semois and demanding additional air cover. Ironically, while the Germans had created a massive traffic jam on that day as their units moved along narrow Ardennes roads, they suffered little interference from the air. Meanwhile, the RAF's Bomber Command followed its doctrine and struck targets in Germany without success instead of supporting the ground campaign in France.

The decisive moment came on 13 May, as three panzer corps established bridgeheads on the far banks of the Meuse. On Guderian's front, the Luftwaffe conducted a three-hour sustained bombardment that broke the back of French artillery support and eventually the entire defensive position. By the morning of 14 May the Germans had bridges across the Meuse and were funnelling tanks across. Attacking Battles and French aircraft suffered horrendous casualties: of seventy-one British bombers attacking on the 14th, the Germans shot down forty (56 per cent). Not a single bomb hit any of the bridges.

By the evening of 15 May German panzer corps had broken through the French positions and were on their way to the Channel. It was here that the Germans gained general air superiority over French territory. The advance captured most of the air bases, with the infrastructure crucial for keeping Allied aircraft in commission and armed. Winston Churchill, Britain's new prime minister, confronted with the collapse of Britain's continental ally, sought to send more fighters to the continent to help defend France. But Fighter Command's leader, Air Chief Marshal Sir Hugh Dowding, resolutely argued against stripping British air defences. His strong stand not only convinced Churchill that he should refuse additional help to the French, but led the great man to defend Dowding that summer against a cabal in the Air Ministry that wanted him removed.

Because they were changing over to a new generation of fighter aircraft the French were running operationally ready rates of 50 per cent or less, a rate similar to those of the Luftwaffe in 1937–8 and the RAF in 1938–9. But the French were now in the middle of a battle for their survival. That they did as well as they did is a tribute to the quality of French pilots and their courage; by the end of the Battle of France, the Luftwaffe had lost nearly 20 per cent of its Bf 109s, 30 per cent of its bombers and dive-bombers, and 40 per cent of its transports. Thus, Fighter Command owed much to the efforts the French Air Force made against the Luftwaffe in the spring of 1940.

The prelude to the Battle of Britain occurred with swirling dogfights in the skies over Dunkirk in late May 1940. There, along the beaches of the Channel coast, Allied forces were desperately attempting to escape as the Wehrmacht closed in. Goering reputedly promised the Führer that the Luftwaffe could prevent Allied forces from escaping, and the Luftwaffe certainly tried to do this. The Germans inflicted substantial damage on the evacuation fleet; they sank or damaged twenty-eight destroyers and torpedo boats. But Spitfires flying out of the United Kingdom inflicted heavy casualties on the Stukas and bombers attacking the evacuation beaches. The air battle over Dunkirk should have sounded a warning klaxon to German air leaders; it did not. Across the board German air planning underestimated British capabilities in early summer 1940. Initial German estimates for an air campaign against Britain were that it would take four days for the Luftwaffe to defeat Fighter Command and only another four weeks to mop up the rest of the RAF. In fact, the Luftwaffe's optimism reflected the mood of euphoria throughout the Third Reich; as the high command's operations officer noted at the end of June, 'the final victory of Germany over England is only a question of time'.

However, the Germans confronted a more formidable opponent than they imagined. The leader of Fighter Command, Hugh Dowding, was one of the most innovative and thoughtful air experts in the interwar period. In 1937 Dowding had taken over Fighter Command and carried through the process of innovation that used technological change to make a complex and effective defensive system. Britain's survival in 1940 rested not only on the technology of fighters and radar, but also on a command and control system that relayed information from the radar stations to the fighters in a matter of minutes, a revival of the defensive system of 1918, but now with improved technology.

The Luftwaffe's underestimation of its opponents was a result not only of Nazi ideology, but also of an appallingly bad intelligence system. On 19 July Colonel Beppo Schmid, chief of Luftwaffe intelligence, reported that British fighters were inferior to the Bf 110 as well as to the Bf 109, failed to mention that the British possessed radar and ended with the observation that 'the Luftwaffe, unlike the RAF, will be in a position in every respect to achieve a decisive effect this

German Dornier Do 17Z medium bombers of KG 76 based at Cormeilles-en-Vexin in France in July 1940, approaching the coast of southern England during the Battle of Britain. Dubbed the 'Flying Pencil', the Do 17 was phased out of front line service by 1942.

year'. In fact, both the British fighters were superior to the Bf 110 – the Spitfire was clearly the equal of the Bf 109, with the Hurricane not far behind. Moreover, in summer 1940 the British began using the American additive tetraethyl lead in their aviation gasoline, which provided approximately a 15 per cent increase in performance. Equally damaging to Luftwaffe prospects was a failure to understand that the British possessed an integrated *system* of air defence, in which the reaction of fighters depended on an effective command and control system. The Luftwaffe stopped bombing radar stations early in the battle; had they understood that the British possessed a complex defence system, they would have realized that the radar stations were the eyes on which British fighters depended.

During July and into early August the Luftwaffe attempted to close the Channel to British shipping. Losses on both sides were heavy, but the British gained a considerable advantage in having a month to work the bugs out of their defensive system. On 11 July, air controllers had scrambled six Hurricanes to meet a 'lone attacker'. What the

Hurricanes discovered, however, was a raid of forty aircraft. After fighting their way back, the pilots, not surprisingly, vented their anger on the controllers. Incidents such as this improved the system when there was relatively little at stake.

Eagle Day (the German code name for the start of operations for the Battle of Britain) got off to a bad start on 13 August. Because of bad weather, the Germans recalled the attacking force, but only the fighters received the message; the bombers flew on, suffered heavy losses and inflicted little damage. Initial German attacks targeted front-line airfields, radar stations and factories supporting the RAF. But the Luftwaffe quickly desisted from its attacks on radar stations, because of its failure to understand the British air defences as a system. The weakness in German intelligence also resulted in a failure to attack the RAF's main production facility for Spitfires (immediately adjacent to the docks at Southampton) until the end of the September – and soon afterwards the day battle would give place to night-time raids, and the Spitfire would become less important. Moreover, the German assumption that Dowding would concentrate his fighters in southern England proved to be wrong. On 15 August, over 100 German bombers escorted by Bf 110s from Norway attacked northern England. The Germans lost nearly 20 per cent of the bombers and failed to attack the intended targets.

Nevertheless, in the second half of August the Germans placed enormous pressure on Fighter Command's structure in southern England. Both sides lost heavily in aircraft and pilots. Attacks on British airfields caused particularly heavy damage. For a time it seemed that the Luftwaffe was pushing Fighter Command to the brink of defeat; even with an infusion of fresh squadrons from the north and the transfer of pilots from other commands, the number of available pilots steadily dropped. But the Luftwaffe was also losing heavily, particularly in bombers, a fact which led Goering to demand that Bf 109s escort bomber formations ever more closely. By now the Luftwaffe had discovered that Bf 110s could not defend themselves, much less protect

Like the Stuka, the Luftwaffe's Messerschmitt Bf 110C long-range fighter had built up a fearsome reputation during the Polish and Low Countries campaigns as a bomber destroyer, but failed disastrously as a bomber escort during the Battle of Britain.

the bombers. Yet Luftwaffe intelligence continued to produce rosy estimates, reporting that Fighter Command was on its last legs. Those actually flying, however, had less reason for optimism. The German ace, Adolf Galland, even told Goering that he would like to have a squadron of Spitfires.

In early September, growing German frustration with the failure to achieve decisive results by attacks on British airfields resulted in a change in German strategy. Goering and Field Marshal Albert Kesselring, one of the war's most overrated commanders, argued that Fighter Command was almost finished and that heavy attacks on London would break the morale of the nation that had failed at Munich. The Führer was delighted at the idea, since he was furious at British bombing raids on Berlin and always inclined to Douhet's idea of attacking enemy morale rather than his air force.

But under Churchill's inspiring leadership, the British were nowhere near cracking. A great daylight raid on 7 September caused vast damage in London's East End. As they had expected continued raids on its infrastructure, Fighter Command was not ready for the attack on London. However, rested by the Luftwaffe's shift to a city-busting approach, British fighters met the next great raid, on 15 September,

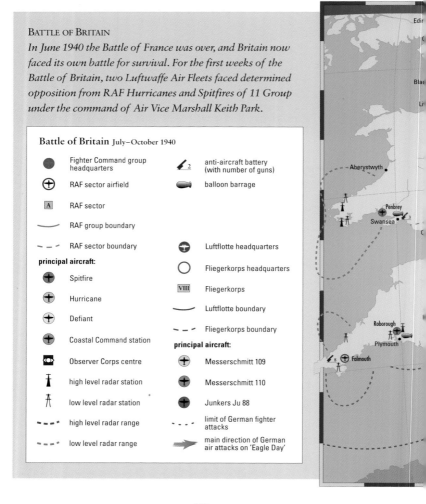

BATTLE OF BRITAIN

In June 1940 the Battle of France was over, and Britain now faced its own battle for survival. For the first weeks of the Battle of Britain, two Luftwaffe Air Fleets faced determined opposition from RAF Hurricanes and Spitfires of 11 Group under the command of Air Vice Marshall Keith Park.

Battle of Britain July–October 1940

- Fighter Command group headquarters
- RAF sector airfield
- A RAF sector
- RAF group boundary
- RAF sector boundary

principal aircraft:
- Spitfire
- Hurricane
- Defiant
- Coastal Command station
- Observer Corps centre
- high level radar station
- low level radar station
- high level radar range
- low level radar range

- 2 anti-aircraft battery (with number of guns)
- balloon barrage

- Luftflotte headquarters
- Fliegerkorps headquarters
- VIII Fliegerkorps
- Luftflotte boundary
- Fliegerkorps boundary

principal aircraft:
- Messerschmitt 109
- Messerschmitt 110
- Junkers Ju 88
- limit of German fighter attacks
- main direction of German air attacks on 'Eagle Day'

Edir

Bla

Li

Aberystwyth

Penbrey

Swansea

Roborough

Plymouth

8 Falmouth

with everything available. Led by intelligence to believe they would meet light resistance, Luftwaffe bomber pilots were taken completely by surprise as Spitfires and Hurricanes slashed through their formations. A substantial number of the crews panicked and dumped their loads

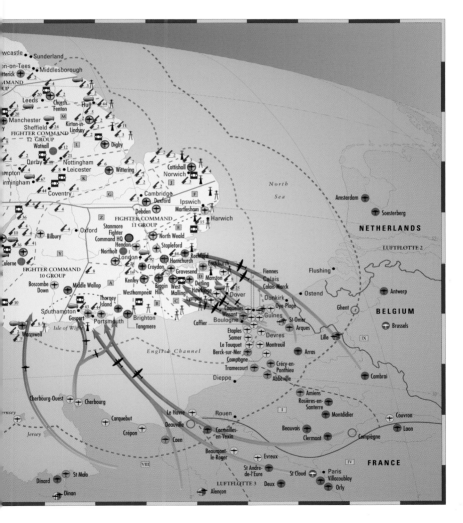

One of the most elegant and effective aircraft of the war, the British Supermarine Spitfire, described by those who flew it as 'a real thoroughbred'. It was the only Allied fighter to remain in continuous production throughout the whole of the Second World War.

over Kent before running. Douglas Bader's wing, based in Duxford, finished the Germans off by arriving in massed force to attack those who carried on to London. While RAF claims exaggerated the enemy losses, the crack in the morale of the bomber crews signalled the Luftwaffe's defeat in daylight battle.

Those who flew Spitfires and Hurricanes in the battle were extraordinarily young, many still in their teens. That, perhaps more than anything explains their resilience in September. They confronted daunting odds and the wounded often paid a terrible price: in escaping from flaming aircraft, many suffered burns that caused excruciating pain, resulted in innumerable operations to repair the damage and scarred them for life. The losses on both sides were heavy: in July Fighter Command lost 10 per cent of its pilots; 26 per cent in August; and 28 per cent in September. (The Luftwaffe figures for fighter pilots over the same period were 11 per cent, 15 per cent, and 23 per cent.)

The story of two pilots encapsulates the tenacity and courage of the victors: Sergeant Josef Frantisek was a Czech who, when the Germans occupied his country in March 1939, flew out to Poland, machine-gunning Nazi columns on the way out. He fought with the Poles in 1939; from there he escaped to France, and then to England. Over the course of September, he shot down seventeen German aircraft, the highest total in Fighter Command during the battle; on 8 October he and his aircraft disappeared while in air-to-air combat over Sussex. The second pilot, Douglas Bader, had joined the RAF during the interwar period and lost both legs in a flying accident. Medically retired, he persuaded the RAF to return him to active duty on the outbreak of war despite his artificial legs; he became a leading ace in the RAF until he was shot down over France in spring 1941. He then spent the rest of the war attempting to escape from POW camps, eventually ending up in the prison fortress, Colditz.

Victory in the daylight battle did not end the assault on Britain. As soon as they had decided to abandon their daytime raids, the Germans began a night offensive, called the Blitz by its victims, to destroy British industry and break British morale. The Luftwaffe was better prepared to conduct such a campaign than Bomber Command: it not only possessed pathfinder units, but the technology to bomb in bad weather or at night with considerable accuracy – with *Knickebein* (a device that utilized radio beams to locate targets).

The day after: London counts the cost.

A retouched photograph of an RAF Supermarine Spitfire Mk 1 attacking a Luftwaffe Dornier Do 17 bomber over Kent during the Battle of Britain in the summer of 1940.

Luckily for British cities, British intelligence, led by the young scientist R. V. Jones, deduced the existence of *Knickebein* in June on the basis of scanty evidence. Jones encountered much doubt among scientists as well as RAF officers, but convinced Churchill of the danger. As a result, the British took increasingly effective counter-measures through the fall and also recognized the introduction of a new blind-bombing device, the *X-Gerät* (dependent on radio pulses). Between September 1940 and March 1941, when Britain stood defenceless at night, their countermeasures reduced the effectiveness of the *Knickebein* beams and thus of the aerial assault. Then, in March, radar-equipped night fighters began to inflict heavy losses on German bombers. The Luftwaffe substantially damaged London, Coventry and ports on the west coast, but failed to break British morale.

One of the most astonishing aspects of the Battle of Britain was how little the participants and observers learned from the experience. For the Germans the battle suggested that air co-operation with the army might offer a more effective way of employing aircraft. The RAF, despite the way British civilians had stood up to bombing, based its approach to strategic bombing on attacking German morale. Moreover, Bomber Command paid very little attention to the problems that the Luftwaffe crews had had in hitting targets accurately even with the support of radio guidance. Arthur Harris, future chief of Bomber Command, commented in the spring of 1941 that he saw no reason for employing blind-bombing technology, since the RAF crews were hitting targets without such devices. (They were not.) The Americans also ignored the battle's implications and aimed at creating a force structure of self-defending bomber fleets with no long-range escort fighters for protection. They argued that German bomber losses had been the result of bad flying discipline, inadequate aircraft and the low altitude at which the Luftwaffe flew. It took two disastrous attacks on Schweinfurt in 1943 to disabuse them of such notions.

There was one issue that the RAF and the US Army Air Force got right and the Luftwaffe wrong: the Battle of Britain underlined the absolute need not only for front-line strength, but for a large production base with an adequate flow of replacement crews. By the second half of 1943 the Americans were turning out 1,000 four-engined bombers per month, while the British produced 600 per month. In the end – ironically in view of the pre-war claims of air theorists – the air war would come to resemble the worst of the First World War's attrition warfare, except that now it was the attrition of expensive machines, officers and aircrew.

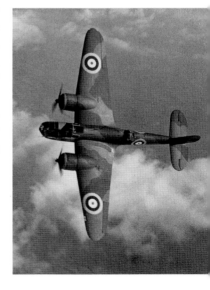

RAF Bomber Command's first modern monoplane bomber, the Bristol Blenheim light bomber, entered service in 1937. The Mk IV, seen here, introduced in 1939, had a range of 1,450 miles and fought in the Battle of France but losses were heavy.

BARBAROSSA AND THE EASTERN FRONT

While the Luftwaffe was preparing for its assault on the British Isles, Hitler and his senior army leaders were planning the destruction of the Soviet Union. By the end of July 1940 the Führer decided to settle accounts with the Soviets in spring 1941. Planning and preparations for the invasion, code-named Operation Barbarossa, proceeded with the inevitability of a Greek tragedy. Barbarossa represented the fulfilment of Nazism's ideological goals to achieve living space and exterminate the racial 'Jewish–Bolshevik' enemy. The assumption underpinning the planning was that the Wehrmacht and the Luftwaffe could destroy the Soviet army and air force along the frontier and then, in Hitler's phrase, 'once the door had been kicked down, the entire structure will collapse like a house of cards'. The Luftwaffe's chief of staff, General Hans Jeschonnek, summed up his service's overconfidence about the upcoming campaign with the remark: 'at last a proper war'.

While planning continued and the Luftwaffe pounded Britain, events in the Mediterranean distracted the Germans. Mussolini had entered the war in June 1940 with seemingly powerful military forces that failed to accomplish anything. In October 1940 the Italians invaded Greece from Albania with completely inadequate preparation. The Italian Air Force attempted to cow the Greeks into surrendering by bombing

After their mauling by RAF fighters during the Battle of Britain, Luftwaffe Messerschmitt Bf 110s were transferred to the Eastern Front and Mediterranean theatres. These Bf 110 C-4s of ZG 1 operated over the Caucasus in 1942.

Athens and other cities, but neither Italian capabilities nor the weather co-operated. A furious Greek population rose up, while the Greek army drove the Italians back into Albania. Encouraged by Italian inaction and Greek resistance, British forces in the Mediterranean went over to the offensive. In November the carrier *Illustrious* launched twenty-one Swordfish biplanes armed with torpedoes to attack Italian battleships in their lair at Taranto. In one of the war's most daring raids, the Swordfish pilots torpedoed and sank half of the Italian battle fleet – one of the three battleships sunk was so badly damaged that the Italians never attempted to repair it. To complete the catalogue of Italian disasters, the British army launched a raid in the desert that rapidly threatened to capture all of the Italian colony of Libya.

Faced with the Italian collapse in Greece, the Germans acted. Covered by the Luftwaffe, the Wehrmacht deployed through Hungary and Romania into Bulgaria so as to attack Greece as soon as the mountain snows melted. Then, in early April, a coup in Yugoslavia overturned the pro-Axis regime. Hitler's response was immediate and brutal. He ordered additional forces to be deployed that would complete Yugoslavia's destruction along with Greece's. Within a week the Germans deployed an additional army to handle Yugoslavia, while an extra 600 aircraft moved from their bases to support the enlarged campaign in the Balkans.

The Luftwaffe now possessed over 1,000 aircraft for forthcoming operations in the Balkans. The first task, however, was not to support the army; as Hitler's directive made clear, the Luftwaffe was to accomplish 'the destruction of Belgrade through a great air attack'. The code name was *Gericht*: punishment. In conformity with the Führer's directive the Germans began bombing Belgrade in the early morning hours in order to start as many fires as possible; bombing continued through the afternoon and into the night, when the massive fires provided excellent marking points. By the time it was over, the assault had killed more than 17,000 civilians, despite the fact that the Yugoslavs had declared Belgrade an open city at the onset of hostilities.

The campaign in Greece and Yugoslavia proceeded at a pace similar to that of the offensive against France and the Low Countries. The Luftwaffe rendered significant support to ground troops by attacking enemy forces and transportation centres as well as providing close air support to the rapidly advancing Wehrmacht troops. By early May it was over. At this point, Hitler decided to complete the campaign with an airborne assault on Crete, where large numbers of British and Commonwealth forces had taken refuge. The plan was simple and straightforward: Luftwaffe paratroopers would seize the airfields at Maleme and Iraklion, and the Luftwaffe would then fly in troops and equipment from the 22nd Mountain Division to complete the operation. This attack was the first time that airborne forces would seize territory without support from land or sea.

There were, however, a number of problems. German intelligence significantly underestimated British and Commonwealth forces on the island. Moreover, unbeknown to the Germans, the British were now reading the Wehrmacht's high-grade ciphers on a regular basis and passing that information, code-named Ultra, to commanders in the Mediterranean. Consequently, General Bernard Freyburg, commander of Crete, received Ultra intelligence on the time and conception of the coming attack. But Freyburg believed that the main effort would come by sea, not by air; consequently, he deployed only one battalion to guard the crucial airfield at Maleme, while the bulk of defending forces guarded beaches and waited for Germans who never came.

After intensive air operations that inflicted little damage on the defenders, German airborne forces struck. The initial landings were a catastrophe. At Iraklion the defenders butchered most of the paratroopers. At Maleme the paratroopers had only gained a toehold on the airfield by the end of the day, despite heavy casualties. That night, the New Zealand battalion commander, whose troops held the hill dominating the airfield, retreated because he had not received any reinforcements. At this point the Germans could finally fly in reinforcements from the 22nd Mountain Division. That sealed Crete's fate. Nevertheless, German losses were so heavy that Hitler never used large-scale airborne forces again; the Allies, however, based their airborne conceptions on the experiences gained in fighting Luftwaffe paratroopers on Crete. Hitler had achieved his aims of shoring up his Italian ally in the Mediterranean, securing Barbarossa's right flank and denying the British Cretan air bases from which to bomb the Romanian oilfields.

With their operations in the Balkans completed, the Wehrmacht's weight fell on the Soviet Union. Some Luftwaffe units, moving from the Balkans, only arrived at their staging areas for Barbarossa in the week prior to the invasion. Despite the momentous tasks confronting the Luftwaffe in the forthcoming campaign, its force structure reflected the strains of the almost continuous fighting over the past year. On 22 June 1941 the Germans had barely 100 fighters more than they had had on 10 May 1940 and 200 *fewer* bombers than a year earlier. In the early hours of 22 June Luftwaffe bomber crews flew over the Soviet–German frontier at high altitude and then dived down to hit Soviet airfields at first light. Caught by surprise despite ample warning, the Soviets desperately attempted to fight back. What ensued was a massacre of Soviet air units, as most still had their aircraft parked wing tip to wing tip. *Fliegerkorps* IV's success on the first day suggests the extent of the

A Luftwaffe Messerschmitt Bf 109G-2 of 4/JG 54, commanded by Major Hannes Trautloft, taxies on a waterlogged airfield at Siverskaya on the northern sector of the Eastern Front in the spring of 1942.

The most widely built version of all the Bf 109 types, the G-Gustav series had a top speed of 403 mph and climbed at almost 4,000 feet per minute. This Bf 109G-6 belongs of JG 54 commanding officer, Major Hannes Trautloft, who shot down forty-five Russian aircraft in 1942–3.

surprise; it reported that it had destroyed 142 enemy aircraft on the ground and only sixteen in the air. For the entire front, Soviet losses totalled 1,200 aircraft in the first eight-and-a-half hours. The desperate situation on the ground forced Soviet commanders to throw air units into battle to stem the German tide. Ill-trained, ill-equipped and ill-prepared, Soviet aircrews floundered in tactically defenceless formations and obsolete aircraft. Field Marshal Erhard Milch, the Luftwaffe's chief of supply, recorded Soviet air losses as 1,800 aircraft on the first day, followed by 800 on 23 June, 557 on the 24th, 351 on the 25th and 300 on the 26th. Since many of these aircraft were obsolete, the real loss was in their crews.

By the end of July the Luftwaffe had run into logistical difficulties similar to those plaguing the army. The support structure delivering fuel and munitions was not adequate for Russia's continental spaces, as opposed to the central European distances to which the Germans were accustomed. As early as 5 July, *Fliegerkorps* VIII's commander, General Wolfram von Richthofen, was noting: 'Supply is the greatest difficulty in this war'. By early August supply difficulties had stalled the ground offensive, while Soviet reserves were putting intense pressure on the German spearheads, particularly around the Yelyna salient.

The Luftwaffe confronted a number of difficulties beyond logistics. The funnel-shaped nature of the theatre meant that aircraft concentration declined drastically as the Luftwaffe moved into Russia's vast spaces. The same thing happened to the ground forces, which increased their calls for air support. In the first months of the invasion the Luftwaffe launched a number of long-range raids against Moscow and Leningrad, but as autumn approached Luftwaffe strength declined and demands from ground forces increased. By autumn the Luftwaffe was launching few attacks on major Soviet cities; moreover, because of the distances and the failure of intelligence as to Soviet industrial strength, the Luftwaffe struck few significant targets behind Moscow.

Luftwaffe units found themselves shuttling back and forth from battlefront to battlefront throughout the late summer and autumn – a situation that only exacerbated supply and maintenance difficulties on the primitive grass fields of the theatre. Visiting bases in the east in the autumn of 1941, Milch discovered a catastrophic situation: aircraft were awaiting repairs at a number of bases, but no work was occurring because the units had moved on and the supply system was providing barely enough bombs, fuel and parts to support operations.

A final drive on Moscow before winter brought the climactic moment of the campaign. Operation Typhoon began in late September and scored spectacular victories against a Soviet high command again caught by surprise. Three panzer armies, supported by more than 1,500 aircraft, slashed through the strung-out Soviet defences. Flying over 1,000 sorties per day, the Luftwaffe was a major factor in the breakthrough. On 5 October Soviet reconnaissance pilots reported a German column over 25 kilometres long driving along the highway between Smolensk and Moscow; the reporting pilots were almost shot for defeatism by the NKVD on their return. In early October the German advance encircled two vast pockets at Bryansk and Vyazma; by the time the fighting had died down, the Germans claimed to have captured over 500,000 enemy soldiers.

But at this point, with the road to Moscow seemingly wide open, the rains arrived turning everything into a morass. On 9 October the Luftwaffe flew only 300 sorties off the sodden grass strips that were its

Heinkel He 111H-16 bombers of KG 53 over the Eastern Front. With a top speed of 232 mph and a payload of 2,200 pounds, these bombers were the backbone of the Luftwaffe medium bomber fleets from 1939–42.

bases. If the Luftwaffe had confronted great difficulties so far, it was now entering a nightmare period. The breakdown in German logistics, exacerbated by a sea of mud, increased demands for Luftwaffe crews to fly in supplies as well as provide direct support to the army. Fog and rain added to the difficulties in finding and hitting targets. Yet so optimistic was the senior leadership that it transferred Field Marshal Kesselring and his *Luftflotte* 2 to the Mediterranean, to restore the deteriorating situation in that theatre.

Only the arrival of cold weather in mid November allowed the ground forces to resume the advance on Moscow. The Luftwaffe, however, was unable to provide much support. Its strength in front of Moscow lay on unimproved airstrips with neither the maintenance nor supply support for sustained operations. The Soviets, however, possessed winter-ready airfields and hangars around Moscow; thus for the first time in the campaign they mounted air operations that provided significant support to the Soviet ground troops. Moreover, Soviet air units were by now receiving newer models from factories in the Urals; consequently, their pilots were flying aircraft that could match Luftwaffe aircraft. In early December the Russian winter brought conditions for which the Germans were completely unprepared, and the Soviet armies went over to the offensive. For the next three months they threatened to destroy the German army on the Eastern Front. The planes the Luftwaffe could still fly became essential to the survival of the hard-pressed ground forces; fighters, long-range bombers, everything was thrown in to supporting the front. By this point the Luftwaffe had become primarily a ground-support force.

But in December 1941 and January 1942, the Luftwaffe was close to collapse. In the first four months of Barbarossa the Luftwaffe lost 36 per cent of its Bf 109 fighter pilots and 56 per cent of its bomber crews. On the maintenance side, the in-commission rate for all Luftwaffe fighters in December 1941 was barely 50 per cent, while the figure for bombers had fallen to 32 per cent. The figures on the Eastern Front were even worse, as Luftwaffe ground crews attempted to repair aircraft in unheated shelters in temperatures well below zero. Admittedly, the Luftwaffe was never in as bad a shape as the army; at least it had the use of its air-transport system to fly winter clothes, parts and lightweight oils to front-line air bases. But in January 1942 less than 15 per cent of its 100,000 vehicles remained in working condition.

By spring, fighting on the Eastern Front had burned itself out; both sides were completely exhausted. Nevertheless, Hitler determined to launch a summer offensive aimed at capturing Stalingrad and at driving deep into the Caucasus to capture and disrupt much of the Soviet Union's oil supplies. Even more than in 1941, the Luftwaffe's role was to support the army's drive with interdiction strikes and close air support. Where the Luftwaffe appeared in strength it could usually dominate the skies. While Soviet equipment had improved noticeably since 1941, Soviet pilots were still not up to the quality of their Luftwaffe opponents – most were rushed to the front with minimal flying training. But the Germans were also hard pressed: new fighter pilots were now serving part of their operational training period in front-line squadrons.

In June 1942 German ground forces, supported by heavy Luftwaffe bombings, captured the naval fortress of Sebastopol. In early July the summer offensive kicked off with a drive to Voronezh and then down the Don. As in 1941, German forces easily broke through Soviet front lines; however, the Red Army rapidly disengaged and retreated into the depths of the southern steppe. There were no more large encirclements of Soviet forces. By the end of August the Germans had reached Stalingrad and moved deep into the Caucasus. Again, the Luftwaffe seemed to have everything its own way, but as the advance continued, the Germans ran into the supply difficulties that had bedeviled them the year before; moreover, ground units, widely dispersed, required increased air support. With its own as well as the army's logistical system in disarray, the Luftwaffe found it increasingly difficult to execute any of its missions effectively.

In late August Hitler's attention swung away from the Caucasus to Stalingrad. Day in and day out the Luftwaffe pounded the city, but tenacious Soviet front-line defences ground down attacking German units and denied them total control of the city. Meanwhile, to the north of Stalingrad, the Soviets carefully screened the deployment of large ground and air forces for a counter-attack aimed at destroying the

EASTERN FRONT DEFEAT
By November 1942 the German Sixth Army was virtually surrounded by Soviet troops and on the 25th the Luftwaffe began an operation to supply it by air. On 16 January 1943, as the Russian winter took a stranglehold on German forces, the Soviets overran the last German-held airfield. The last air drop to the doomed Sixth Army took place on 3 February by which time the Luftwaffe had lost more than 250 Ju 52 transports.

Stalingrad airlift
September 1942-February 1943

→ German airlift

— German front lines

— limit of Russian artillery

N

German Sixth Army. At last, in the summer of 1942 Soviet industry was producing significant numbers of modern fighters and bombers. And the Soviet high command had husbanded much of this production to support the forthcoming offensive. As was to be the case throughout the remainder of the war, Soviet deception cast a veil over these preparations.

Thus, the Soviet counter-attack on the flanks of the Stalingrad salient, begun on 19 November, caught the Germans by surprise. On both flanks, supported by massive numbers of aircraft, the Soviets achieved a clean breakthrough. The German high command proved incapable of making a quick decision – Hitler wasted two days travelling to his headquarters in East Prussia from Berchtesgaden, while senior army leaders, including those in command of the Sixth Army, believed that the Luftwaffe could support Stalingrad by airlift. Luftwaffe leaders on the spot had no such illusions; General Wolfram von Richthofen, Manfred's cousin, warned that under the conditions of winter such an

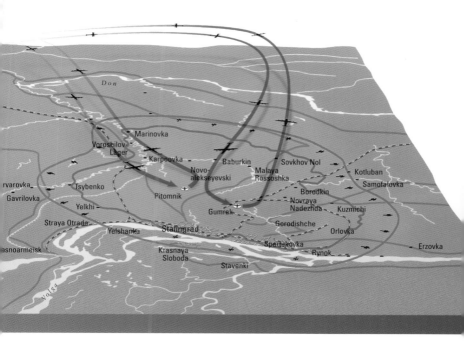

airlift was technically impossible. In East Prussia, however, Goering promised the Führer that the Luftwaffe could do the impossible. What made such a promise even more bizarre was the fact that at that precise moment many of the Luftwaffe's transports were flying paratroopers and ground forces over to North Africa to seize Tunisia.

The Soviets initially concentrated on ensuring that the German Sixth Army would not escape. Thus, much of their effort focused on disrupting the air bridge into Stalingrad, while large anti-aircraft forces moved forward into the area controlling access to the pocket. Already the Russian winter had descended on to the steppe outside Stalingrad. The Germans flew from two airfields at Morozovskaya and Tatsinkaya; from the first, the resupply operation had an air of improvisation. The Luftwaffe could only provide crews and aircraft by stripping training units of instructors, aircraft and, in some cases, students. Those in charge of the supply operation were neither trained nor prepared for their task: the first Ju 52 arrived in the pocket with a load of prophylactics.

The winter conditions again created a maintenance nightmare that drove in-commission rates down to less than 20 per cent. Soviet fighters and anti-aircraft guns took a rising toll of aircraft flying into the pocket, while Luftwaffe fighter pilots fought a losing battle to protect the transports. The army estimated that the garrison needed an aerial delivery of 660 tons per day. On only three days of the airlift did totals reach 300 tons, while the daily average hovered around 100 tons. In response to the airlift and German efforts to reach the pocket, the Soviets launched a major offensive along the upper Don. On 24 December Soviet armour overran Tatsinkaya, with many German aircraft escaping just as the Soviets reached the airfield boundary. The Soviets also brought Morozovskaya under artillery fire. By early January the Germans had lost this as well, making aerial supply of the pocket almost impossible.

But the Germans had other worries as well. The breakthrough along the Don threatened to put all of Army Group South in the bag. For one of the last times in the war Hitler deferred to military advice and

A transport version of the Focke-Wulf Condor long-range reconnaissance bomber, the Fw 200C-4/U1, was used by high-ranking officers and on the Eastern Front during the ill-fated Stalingrad airlift in the winter of 1942/3.

allowed the forces in the Caucasus to retreat, while Manstein, commander of Army Group South, made a brilliant effort to pull German forces back from the Don without another catastrophe. In February, the Soviets outran their supply lines and air support, while the Germans, who were falling back on their supply lines, regenerated sufficient air and ground forces to launch a counter-attack. The German counterblow came at the end of the month. It combined Richthofen's close air-support units with Manstein's panzers to destroy significant Soviet armoured forces and recapture the city of Kharkov. It was to be the last air–ground success of German arms in the Second World War.

Once again the miserable conditions of spring rain and mud brought military operations to an end on both sides of the line. The Germans confronted the same strategic problem that had confronted them in early 1942: the threat from Anglo-American power was growing, while something had to be done to reduce Soviet military capabilities before Anglo-American forces returned to the continent. But now Allied air operations were inflicting serious damage on Axis forces, not only in the Mediterranean but also in Germany itself. Throughout the autumn of 1942 approximately 60 per cent of German air power had been deployed on the Eastern Front; now, however, air operations against the RAF and US Army Air Force were drastically changing that ratio.

After rejecting other alternatives, Hitler decided to attack Soviet forces in the salient around Kursk. What had seemed like a promising operation in the spring became increasingly dubious as the Führer delayed the start of Operation Citadel to ensure everything was ready. The delay ensured that the Soviets were also ready, in the air as well as on the ground. When the Germans began their offensive against the Kursk salient, they ran into thoroughly prepared enemy defences. But the Soviet air effort began badly; an attempt to strike German airfields near Kharkov that were crowded with aircraft misfired at the beginning of the battle. German radar picked up the approaching Soviet bombers and Luftwaffe fighters slaughtered the attackers. But Kursk proved a terrible grinding battle. Early in the fighting, the Germans gained local superiority, but as it continued Soviet numbers exercised an increasing influence. Moreover, Soviet skill levels were improving; on 6 July Ivan N. Kozhedub, who was to be the leading Soviet ace of the war with sixty-two confirmed kills, made his first combat patrol and barely survived. But by the end of the battle he had shot down two Ju 87s and two Bf 109s. The Luftwaffe found it difficult to maintain its initial level of effort, while Soviet aircraft increasingly intervened in the ground battle. Losses on both sides were heavy, but, given the pressures in other theatres, the Luftwaffe was in no position to replace its losses, while the Soviets were.

A series of massive Soviet offensives, all heavily supported by Soviet air units, followed the German defeat at Kursk. The Red Army drove the Germans back and over the Dnepr. The Luftwaffe played an increasingly peripheral role in the fighting as much of its strength, particularly in fighters, was transferred back to the Reich to meet the daylight bombing offensive of the US Eighth Air Force. And while individual German pilots, such as Eric Hartmann, accumulated vast totals of Soviet aircraft destroyed, the Luftwaffe became almost irrelevant as a factor in the fighting in the east for the remainder of the war. The same situation prevailed on other fronts; the weary battered German ground forces rarely if ever saw Luftwaffe aircraft.

Soviet Ilyushin Il-2M-3 Shturmovik ground attack aircraft, bearing the banner 'Avenger', over the outskirts of Berlin in 1945. Armed with two 37mm cannon, two 7.62mm machine-guns and one 12.7mm cannon, it was a formidable close air support aircraft.

For the Luftwaffe, the campaign in the east had been a frustrating affair. It had achieved stunning success in the first days of Barbarossa, but after that had found itself sucked into a campaign of supporting the army. In fact, the strained situation on the ground increasingly prevented the Luftwaffe from attacking the industrial infrastructure of the Soviet Union even in the immediate region of Moscow. And that industrial infrastructure, almost entirely undisturbed, provided the regeneration of Soviet air strength in such numbers that by 1943, even without commitments elsewhere, the Luftwaffe confronted increasing difficulties in controlling even its own air space. Moreover, in 1942, the Luftwaffe, concentrating on supporting the ground battles in the Caucasus and at Stalingrad, probably missed a significant opportunity to strike the Soviet oil industry around Baku. Had they done so, the Germans might have considerably hindered the Red Army's long-term potential to conduct mobile operations.

THE WAR AT SEA

While the Eastern Front saw the blunting of Nazi Germany's drive on the ground, Britain, the United States and Canada waged a deadly war against the U-boat in the battle of the Atlantic. In many respects that effort was the most important campaign of the Second World War, since on its success depended the ability of Britain and the United States to project military power, land as well as air, on to the European continent. However, the battle of the Atlantic possessed none of the clarity that most military history possesses. As Churchill underlined, it was a war of graphs and tonnages. Air power's greatest contribution lay not in the number of U-boats sunk, but rather in the endless patrols that forced U-boat shadowers to submerge, and prevented the concentration of Admiral Karl Dönitz's wolf-packs around convoys carrying the lifeblood of America's military and economic power. The most successful convoys were those not attacked at all.

Air power played a crucial, if not decisive, role in that struggle. Yet in spite of its contribution to the defeat of the U-boat in the First World War, the British were surprisingly slow to bring air power to the new struggle. Part of the problem lay in the fact that, until 1942, Coastal Command remained a backwater for the RAF; but the Royal Navy was not at all air-minded in addressing the submarine threat. Adding to British problems was the Chamberlain government's surrender of British rights to bases on Ireland's west coast, an action which added substantially to the distance that convoy escorts had to travel and limited the range of British aircraft flying out into the central Atlantic.

The German conquest of France in 1940 altered the geography of the U-boat war to Germany's advantage, especially in comparison to the First World War. It allowed U-boats to reach out farther and more quickly into the Atlantic; and it provided the Luftwaffe with bases for long-range aircraft, the Focke-Wulf 200 Condor. Luckily for the British, Goering and the Luftwaffe high command displayed little interest in supporting the navy in the battle of the Atlantic. Nevertheless, the German admiralty had been no more enthusiastic before the war than

The Focke-Wulf Fw 200C Condor long-range maritime reconnaissance bomber was developed from a civil transport aircraft. With a range of 2,175 miles, Fw 200C-4s of KG 40, based at Bordeaux-Merignac, became the scourge of Allied Atlantic convoys during 1941.

the Royal Navy about using aircraft to support a naval war. The savage attacks on British convoys in the autumn of 1940 awoke both sides to the possibilities. But in 1940 the Germans had too few submarines to win the battle, while the Royal Navy possessed far too few escorts.

One thing, however, was clear from the first: aircraft were essential. At a minimum, the presence of aircraft forced U-boats to submerge and thus lose contact with the convoys. Where patrol aircraft could not reach, U-boats could shadow convoys and call in the wolf-packs. As the battle moved into the central Atlantic during the winter of 1940/41, the Condors played a major role in German successes, both by attacking convoys directly and in providing reconnaissance. For the British, the need to reach as far into the Atlantic as possible to provide air cover was apparent from early 1941. But the RAF obdurately refused to allow diversion of any four-engined bomber production (including American aid) to the battle of the Atlantic.

Over the second half of 1941, the Royal Navy deflected the U-boat threat with the aid of Ultra decrypts of German message traffic. This intelligence coup allowed the Western Approaches Command to move convoys around U-boat concentrations and to reduce drastically losses due to U-boats. But in January 1942 the situation swung back in favour of Dönitz. The addition of another rotor to the U-boat Enigma encoding machines prevented the British from continuing to read the German message traffic, while the entrance of a completely unprepared

United States into the war provided a rich new hunting-ground for the U-boats. Despite the availability of airfields up and down the East Coast and throughout the Caribbean, the Americans gave little air support to merchant shipping and were not even prepared to convoy it. For the next six months German submarines enjoyed what they called a second 'happy time'. Nevertheless, by the late summer of 1942 US anti-submarine work, supported by naval aircraft, had driven the U-boats back into the central Atlantic.

In the far reaches of the Arctic in the summer of 1942, the Germans won a temporary victory over Arctic convoys to Murmansk. The triple threat of Luftwaffe aircraft, U-boats and surface warships was sufficient to shut down the convoys after inflicting catastrophic losses, particularly on convoy PQ 17. But again the Luftwaffe was not willing or able to put sufficient resources into the anti-shipping mission; and in November

BATTLE OF THE ATLANTIC
After almost losing the Battle of the Atlantic to German U-boats in 1941, the advent of new long-range American aircraft such as the Catalina and Liberator with new weapons (including the Mk 24 torpedo with an acoustic head) assigned to RAF Coastal Command, the U-boat menace had been broken by Allied air power by the end of 1944.

MEXICO
US
Berm
CUBA
HAITI
Colon
DOM. REP.
COLOMBIA
VENEZUELA
BRAZIL

| 0 | 500 km |
| 0 | 500 miles |

Battle of the Atlantic
1942–45

→ Allied shipping routes
--- limit of Allied air patrols 1942
--- limit of Allied air patrols 1945
⊥ area of U-boat activity

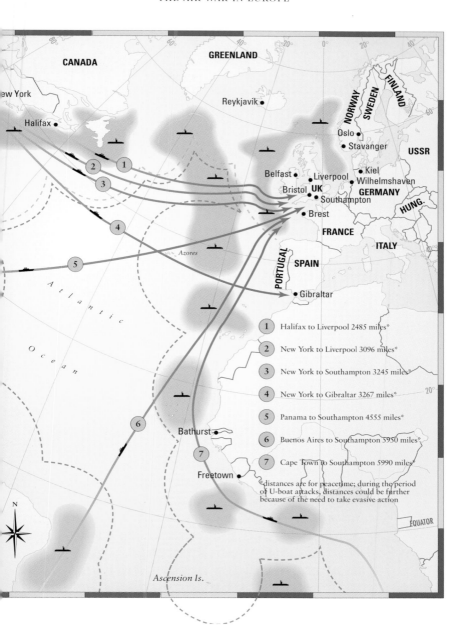

CANADA

GREENLAND

ew York

Halifax

NORWAY

SWEDEN

FINLAND

Reykjavik

Oslo

Stavanger

USSR

Belfast

Liverpool

Kiel

Wilhelmshaven

Bristol

UK

GERMANY

Southampton

HUNG.

Brest

FRANCE

ITALY

Azores

PORTUGAL

SPAIN

Gibraltar

A t l a n t i c

O c e a n

1 Halifax to Liverpool 2485 miles*

2 New York to Liverpool 3096 miles*

3 New York to Southampton 3245 miles*

4 New York to Gibraltar 3267 miles*

5 Panama to Southampton 4555 miles*

6 Buenos Aires to Southampton 5950 miles*

7 Cape Town to Southampton 5990 miles*

*distances are for peacetime; during the period
of U-boat attacks, distances could be further
because of the need to take evasive action

Bathurst

Freetown

N

Ascension Is.

EQUATOR

An RAF Catalina I anti-submarine flying boat of No 209 Squadron based at Castle Archdale in 1941. With an endurance of eighteen hours, RAF Consolidated Catalinas patrolled the Atlantic and Indian Oceans with two of their captains being awarded the VC.

the Germans shifted the Luftwaffe's anti-shipping aircraft from northern Norway to the Mediterranean to attack Allied shipping supporting the 'Torch' landings. By the autumn of 1942 the focus was back on the central Atlantic. With nearly double the number of submarines they had in 1941, the Germans inflicted heavy damage on the convoys they located. In Britain the air staff still refused to loosen its grip on four-engined bombers, while US Army Air Force leaders were no more forthcoming with their bomber production. Yet the figures overwhelmingly supported naval arguments: where long-range aircraft provided cover, the U-boat was not a significant danger. Where they did not, namely in the gap between coverage from Iceland and Newfoundland, U-boats still inflicted heavy losses. But the defending navies, eventually equipped with escort carriers and long-range aircraft, were able to concentrate air power directly on threatened convoys.

The battle of the Atlantic reached its climax in the spring of 1943. In March 1943, with the mid-Atlantic gap in air coverage still remaining, U-boats sank close to 700,000 tons of Allied shipping. Two months later, with long-range coverage available, the gap closed, and with the appearance of significant numbers of escort carriers Allied anti-submarine forces turned the table on the Germans. In May the Allies sank forty-one U-boats – nearly as many as Allied naval forces had sunk in the whole of the first three years of the war.

THE MEDITERRANEAN

Denied access to Continental Europe by France's collapse in 1940, Britain and eventually the United States had to concentrate their efforts in the Mediterranean. In the long run this strategic reality allowed the Anglo-American powers to build up their capabilities, numbers and battlefield knowledge to the point where they could confront the Wehrmacht more equally. The British recognized the advantages of a Mediterranean strategy; the Americans had to be dragged into committing themselves to that theatre. Air power played a number of important roles in the Mediterranean. It proved particularly useful in the defence of Malta and in reaching out from that island to attack Rommel's supply lines to Libya. When RAF capabilities provided a modicum of protection to Malta, Allied air and sea power devastated Axis convoys. When, however, the Luftwaffe turned the tables on the British, as with the arrival of Kesselring's *Luftflotte 2* in November 1941, Rommel's supplies arrived with few losses. Thus, the air situation on Malta had a direct and palpable influence on the course of ground operations in Libya and Egypt.

In the desert the RAF was under the command of one of the most innovative and imaginative commanders of the Second World War, Air Marshal Arthur Tedder. He proved an apt student of the actual conditions of war. The RAF in the Middle East gave priority to tasks which the air staff had regarded with disdain throughout the interwar period: first, it would gain air superiority; second, it would attack Axis supply lines; and third, it would support the army in its ground battles with the *Afrikakorps*. Deployment of British air power to the Mediterranean involved a great logistic system that flew aircraft across the great expanses of central Africa and then up the Nile valley.

Under Tedder's leadership the RAF proved an innovative and effective instrument of military power in the Mediterranean theatre. But no matter how effective it was, air power could not make up for the severe deficiencies in British army doctrine, training and intellectual preparation. The results showed all too clearly in the Gazala battles of May and June 1942; air power alone could not override the British army's incompetence and the German army's battle effectiveness. Moreover, in the spring of 1942 the Luftwaffe had sufficient resources in theatre to contest with the RAF directly over the battlefield. Nevertheless, claims on both sides were at times dubious.

The appearance of Bernard Law Montgomery, one of the nastiest but most effective generals of the war, ushered in a new era in RAF–army co-operation. Montgomery understood the value of co-operation with the RAF, and Tedder fully supported his subordinates in developing it. By collocating his headquarters with Montgomery's, Air Vice Marshal Arthur Alan Conningham, commander of RAF ground support forces in the theatre, provided the desert army with unheard-of responsiveness. But Tedder also understood the need for a wider air campaign to drive the Luftwaffe from the skies and to prevent the arrival of the supplies on which the *Afrikakorps* depended.

An artist's impression of a British Malta convoy under a mass German air attack by Ju 87 Stukas in the Mediterranean in 1942.

It was air power in its widest applications that helped the Eighth Army overcome the *Afrikakorps*'s battle effectiveness at El Alamein in late October 1942. Even before the battle, the RAF had severely damaged Rommel's supply lines across the Mediterranean and disrupted movement between ports in Libya and the front line. Equally important, RAF fighters established air superiority, so that the air commanders could concentrate the RAF on impeding the movement of Rommel's forces and on support of the ground battle. Montgomery's victory was quite different from early British victories in the desert. In a sustained battle of attrition in which air power provided direct support as well as interdiction strikes for Commonwealth troops, Montgomery's Eighth Army broke the *Afrikakorps*, first by denying it mobility and then by fighting the battle on British terms. El Alamein heralded the bold stroke of Anglo-American sea power, Operation Torch, against French North Africa – a strike which occurred on the far side of the African continent from Egypt.

Hitler replied to Torch by flying paratroopers over to seize Tunisia and then following up with major reinforcements – far larger forces than those he had denied Rommel in the summer of 1942. Rommel's retreat across Libya was sufficiently skilled to get his forces to Tunisia

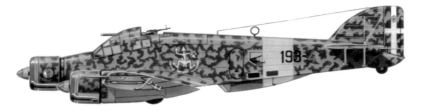

Another Axis bomber developed from a civil transport was the Italian Savoia-Marchetti SM.79 Sparviero. The three-engine SM.79, this example served with the 30th Stormo in Sicily in 1941, was deployed to every theatre where Italian forces operated.

and to launch a surprise attack in January 1943 on the exposed and ill-trained American forces at the Kasserine Pass before the British caught up from the east. Moreover, the Luftwaffe gave Allied air forces in Algeria serious trouble, while the arrangements between air and ground in Algeria were considerably behind the procedures that the desert air force and army had already worked out.

In fact, the reinforcing Axis forces in Tunisia were in an impossible strategic position. Once Allied air forces had sorted themselves out, they imposed a stranglehold on Axis supply lines. Ultra decrypts provided detailed intelligence of the movement of those supplies by sea and air; by the end of March, Allied air attacks had closed down the movement of shipborne supplies. The Luftwaffe then made a desperate attempt in April and early May to supply hard-pressed Axis troops by an aerial bridge, but this was no more successful than the Stalingrad effort. The results were even more devastating, as Allied fighter forces, alerted by decrypts, consistently intercepted and decimated transport formations. But Axis leadership in the theatre did not do much to help; Johannes Steinhoff, the great German ace, travelling through Italy in early 1943 on his way to take up command in Tunisia, was astonished by the luxury and comfort of Kesselring's staff. The great man himself, according to Steinhoff's memoirs, was completely out of touch with combat conditions and was sickeningly optimistic. Ultra decrypts indicated that Kesselring was pressing his fighter pilots throughout the battle to act with the fanaticism of the Japanese. Not surprisingly, the Luftwaffe suffered casualties that it could not afford.

German troubles in the theatre were, however, only beginning. With the collapse of the Tunisian pocket, Allied air forces turned their attention to destroying German and Italian air power throughout Sicily and southern Italy in preparation for Operation Husky – the code name for the invasion of Sicily. By now Allied aircraft based in North Africa were attacking industrial targets in northern Italy. The response of US air commanders in the Mediterranean to actual combat conditions indicates that they were better able to adapt in that theatre than was the case in England. As early as May 1943, Major-General James Doolittle, commander of the Twelfth Air Force in the Mediterranean, was warning General Hap Arnold, commander of the US Army Air Force, that large formations of heavy bombers would not survive against strong Luftwaffe opposition unless accompanied by long-range escort fighters.

The preparation for the invasion of Sicily in July 1943 and that of Italy in September 1943 precipitated the last great air battles in the Mediterranean. By now, the Luftwaffe was unable to stand up to Allied numbers. In his depressing memoirs covering the fighting over Sicily, Steinhoff records the terrible pressure on German fighter squadrons, where the new pilots died almost immediately, while the experienced simply lasted a bit longer. For a loss of over 1,000 aircraft in July and August, the Luftwaffe achieved little but to deplete further its own force structure and make it less able to withstand the swelling pressure of the Combined Bomber Offensive.

THE DEFEAT OF THE LUFTWAFFE
The effort to destroy Nazi Germany's industrial potential and civilian morale by strategic bombing had begun with the unleashing of Bomber Command by the British government in May 1940 in response to the invasion of western Europe. The bomber offensive produced little for the next two-and-a-half years despite extravagant claims by its

supporters. The Butt Report, an analysis of mission photographs in the summer of 1941, indicated that only one in five aircrews were dropping their bombs within five miles of the target – and the target area was no less than seventy-five square miles! Only the fact that Britain had no other means of striking Nazi Germany kept the bomber campaign alive. Moreover, not until Arthur Harris took over Bomber Command in February 1942 did the bomber offensive receive the leadership it required.

Harris had a simple conception: under the cover of night, British bombers in large enough numbers would destroy German cities one after another until civilian morale in Nazi Germany collapsed. In fact, until the end of 1943 the technology was not available to do anything more than attack cities. Harris dedicated himself single-mindedly to the creation of such a force. Even with new bombers, technological support (something that RAF commanders were not interested in until they confronted defeat) and improved techniques, Bomber Command failed to inflict sustained and effective damage on the Germans until early 1943. By that time Harris's forces had sufficient strength to batter the Ruhr in a series of damaging raids.

The Short Stirling was the first but least successful of the RAF long-range heavy bombers. Overweight and under-armed, the Stirling's low ceiling contributed to its heavy losses. This Stirling B.1 of No 149 Squadron at Lakenheath in 1942 was replaced by the Lancaster a year later.

In July 1943 Harris turned to Hamburg. In a devastating series of raids Bomber Command came into its own as a city-busting force. The second attack on 27 July was particularly effective. Admittedly, conditions were perfect. Hamburg was easily identified by airborne radar; the city had not received much rain over the past several months; the weather was hot and dry; the British used Window (aluminum strips which clouded large sections of German radar coverage) to blind German radar for the first time; much of Hamburg's fire-fighting force was well away from the centre of the city, dealing with smouldering coal and coke fires on the city's outskirts; and the first pathfinders put their markers down in the middle of the largest timber yard in Europe, thereby making further marking superfluous. Within a matter of minutes a great firestorm had started, which succeeding crews added to with their bomb loads. As the super-heated air rose with the smoke and cinders over the dying city, air from the outside rushed into the vacuum. After the raid German experts estimated that winds reached in excess of 300 miles per hour and temperatures in some parts of the city may have reached 1,000 degrees. Hamburg's dead in the raid numbered between 30,000 and 40,000.

When German armaments minister Albert Speer heard the results he warned Hitler that six more raids on such a scale would 'bring armaments production to a halt'. But Bomber Command was incapable of replicating Hamburg except under perfect conditions. The Hamburg raid did have a severe impact on German morale, as did other raids on other cities throughout the year, as reports by the secret police underlined. But it was one thing to affect German morale and another thing to persuade Germans to rise against the Nazi regime – especially against a regime that had displayed extraordinary ruthlessness against its enemies from its assumption of power. That, in a nutshell, was the problem with much of airpower theory: modern totalitarian regimes are capable of dealing with almost any threat, except the actual occupation of their territory by enemy troops.

The Avro Lancaster was the best heavy bomber of the European war. Entering service with Bomber Command in 1942, the Lancaster, powered by four Rolls-Royce Merlin engines, equipped no less than fifty-six front line RAF squadrons which flew 156,000 sorties dropping a total of 608,000 tons of bombs. This Lancaster B I belongs to No. 50 Squadron based at Skellingthorpe in Lincolnshire.

Bewitched by his success in disarming German defences in the summer of 1943, Harris determined to destroy Berlin. Beginning in November, Bomber Command began a campaign that forced its aircraft to fly right across Germany to attack Berlin, but the city's mass and geographic position made it difficult to achieve the bombing concentrations that had destroyed Hamburg. Two additional factors made the task more difficult. First, winter weather made it difficult to achieve bombing concentrations and prevented reconnaissance of the results until February 1944. Secondly, the autumn of 1943 German defences were recovering from Window's impact. The introduction of new radar sets in the night-fighter force rendered useless much of the veil that Window had provided. But equally important was the fact that the Luftwaffe had introduced a new system that allowed for the feeding of night fighters directly into the bomber stream.

Throughout the winter of 1943–4, Harris drove his crews hard. The leader of Bomber Command's pathfinders, Air Marshal D. C. Bennett, commented after the war that the battle of Berlin 'had been the worst thing that could have happened to the Command'. There was no corresponding increase in effectiveness, while crew losses steadily mounted. In November 1943 losses had been surprisingly low, less than 4 per cent, but in retrospect this was largely the result of the appallingly bad weather. Thereafter, bomber losses skyrocketed. In December the sortie loss rate climbed to 6.1 per cent (162 bombers); in January to 7.2 per cent (316 bombers). Defeat came on the night of 30–31 March when the Germans shot down 108 bombers attacking Nuremberg; the Halifaxes of No. 4 Group had a particularly bad night, losing 20 bombers or 20.6 per cent of the aircraft they dispatched. To all intents and purposes Bomber Command's single-minded pursuit of German urban destruction had come to a screeching halt. Harris now had to turn to supporting the invasion of Europe – a task he fought against tooth and nail, but to which political and military forces drove him. The cost of the offensive thus far in the war underlines how far off the mark pre-war theorists had been in their claims that air war would prevent a repeat of the First World War's terrible losses in the trenches: between January 1943 and March 1944, Bomber Command lost 5,881 bombers, with most of their crews.

The Americans had arrived with their B-17 Flying Fortresses in the early summer of 1942, but their numbers and training were insufficient to risk raids into German territory. Consequently, the Eighth Air Force limited its efforts to raids against French industrial targets that were supporting the Nazi war economy. Where these raids occurred within range of escort fighter support, B-17s suffered 'acceptable' losses, but where the targets lay beyond the range of such support, losses climbed to over 6 per cent, an unacceptable level. The diversion of US air power in Europe to the Mediterranean, to support Operation Torch, put off the time when American airmen would test their theory of precision, daylight bombing.

The Boeing B-17 Fortress was the spearhead of the American bombing offensive in Europe from the beginning to the end, as well as serving in every other theatre of the war. This pair of USAAF B-17E Forts were deployed to England as part of the Eighth Air Force in 1942.

The testing began in late spring 1943 as Lt. Gen. Ira Eaker, the Eighth's commander, achieved sufficient strength to attack targets in Germany. As US bomber formations reached deeper into Germany, they met furious opposition from the Luftwaffe. From the first, losses reached high levels. In May the Eighth suffered the loss of 37.6 per cent of the crews who had been on active duty at the month's beginning; in June 38.3 per cent; in July 34.7 per cent; in August 31.3 per cent; and no less than 37.4 per cent in October. In the main, the Eighth concentrated on Luftwaffe factories and on the ball-bearing industry. In the case of the former, it achieved some significant, but not decisive results. German construction of new (not reconditioned or repaired aircraft, both of which were counted in the figures to which historians normally refer) single-engine fighters dropped by 24 per cent between July and December.

The ball-bearing industry appeared an even more vulnerable target, because factories in the Schweinfurt produced nearly 55 per cent of the Reich's supply. The 1943 raids on Schweinfurt appeared to do substantial damage, but post-war analysis underlined the faults in the linear approach that pre-war air-power theorists had taken. Although bombs knocked down the roofs and walls of the factories, the machine tools that made the ball-bearings received relatively little damage. Moreover, Speer discovered that most German factories already held substantial reserves of ball-bearings, that roller bearings could in many instances serve as replacements and that the mercenary Swedes and Swiss were delighted to supply the Nazi war machine with what was needed to keep it running, of course for a price.

The first attack on Schweinfurt was combined with a raid on Regensburg. The losses from the two attacks came to 60 bombers; two months later the Eighth went back and lost another 60 bombers over Germany (17 more were written off upon return, while 121 more were damaged, but reparable). In fact, the second Schweinfurt raid was a bad day in a bad week. From 8 October to 14 October the Eighth Air Force lost 148 bombers out of a force structure that averaged 763 bombers over the course of the month (19 per cent). The root of the problem lay in the fact that even with drop tanks, US fighters could barely reach over the Rhine (British fighters had substantially shorter range). Behind the

A formation of USAAF Eighth Air Force B-17G Fortresses of the 533rd Bomb Squadron/381st Bomb Group on a daylight raid over Europe in late 1944 escorted by a Ninth Air Force P-47 Thunderbolt fighters in the background.

Rhine the Luftwaffe could marshal its daytime single-engined day fighters as well as its night fighters. Like the senior RAF leaders who in the early 1940s had argued that long-range fighters were technologically unfeasible, American airmen simply ignored the possibility of providing long-range fighter support. Not until the second Schweinfurt attack did

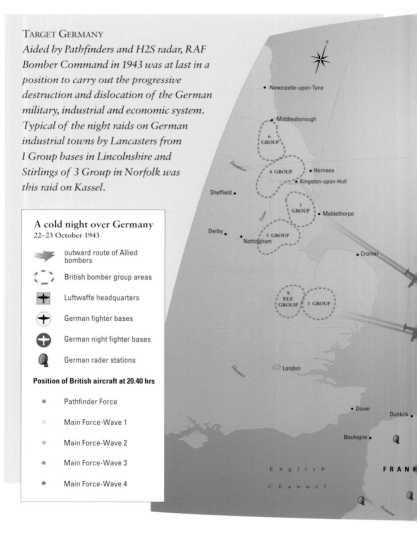

TARGET GERMANY
Aided by Pathfinders and H2S radar, RAF Bomber Command in 1943 was at last in a position to carry out the progressive destruction and dislocation of the German military, industrial and economic system. Typical of the night raids on German industrial towns by Lancasters from I Group bases in Lincolnshire and Stirlings of 3 Group in Norfolk was this raid on Kassel.

A cold night over Germany
22–23 October 1943

— outward route of Allied bombers

— British bomber group areas

✚ Luftwaffe headquarters

✈ German fighter bases

✈ German night fighter bases

◗ German rader stations

Position of British aircraft at 20.40 hrs

● Pathfinder Force

● Main Force-Wave 1

● Main Force-Wave 2

● Main Force-Wave 3

● Main Force-Wave 4

Eaker push energetically for such fighters; even the American drop-tank programme, to extend the range of P-38s and P-47s, was in disarray.

If the Americans and the British were having difficulties in waging the Combined Bomber Offensive, the Germans were in even worse shape. The decision to fight three great air battles – in the east, in the

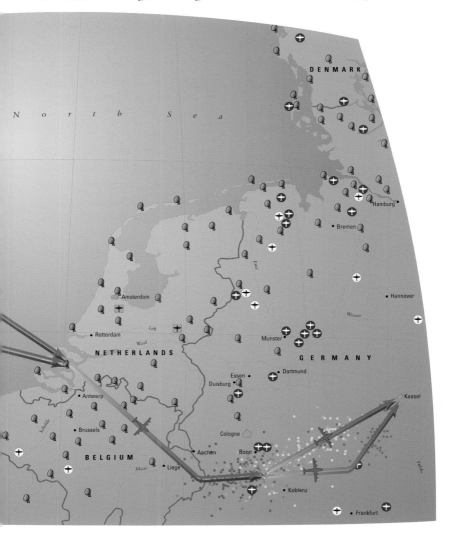

Mediterranean, and over the Reich – in July and August 1943 had resulted in catastrophic losses: well over 1,000 aircraft in each theatre. The pressures on the Luftwaffe, combined with these results, were sufficient for Jeschonnek, the Luftwaffe's chief of staff, to blow his brains out on 18 August, the morning after the Eighth Air Force had attacked Schweinfurt and Bomber Command had blasted the rocket development station of Peenemünde. The pressure of the Combined Bomber Offensive on the Reich itself forced the Luftwaffe's leaders to concentrate their forces on the defence of Germany itself. Yet the political leadership, and in particular Hitler himself, refused to recognize the seriousness of the situation. To the end the Führer remained a disciple of Douhet in his conception of air power. Despite the growing air threat in the west, he and Goering had emphasized production of bombers over fighters. Night fighters received the lowest priority of all, while the anti-aircraft force continued to expand at a rapid rate despite the fact that the Germans knew that it was an ineffective weapon. Nevertheless, because it provided substantial psychological support to Germany's hard-pressed civilian population – the sound of the guns blasting into the night air did suggest that the Nazi government was doing something to protect its citizens – Hitler poured resources into a system that was costly in terms of manpower and arms production, and which could have played a more effective role in the ground battle.

The Luftwaffe now took a number of steps that improved the air situation in the short run. The night fighters moved from a defence based on GCI (ground control intercept) stations where one radar station controlled one fighter, to a system that directed the radar-equipped fighters into the bomber stream rather than against individual bombers. Equipped with new radar that mitigated the effects of Window, German night fighters took a heavy toll of British bombers – a toll that culminated in the slaughter of the Nuremberg raid in late March 1944. The concentration of day fighters back on German soil enabled the air force to survive the increasingly strong pressure from the American bomber offensive. But throughout the

The Liberator had an impressive range enabling it to undertake deep daylight penetration raids, but nothing could protect it from accurate flak. Here a B-24D of the 491st Bomb Group is chopped in two by German anti-aircraft fire, in 1944, deep over occupied Europe.

summer and the autumn of 1943 it was touch and go. Although American bomber crews wildly exaggerated their successes against German fighters, they did shoot down substantial numbers of German fighters. For example, during the August Schweinfurt/Regensburg raid, the Germans lost 24 single-engined fighters and two Bf 110s shot down, with 12 more fighters written off due to battle damage and 25 more damaged but reparable. The pressures the Luftwaffe fighter force was under is suggested by the fact that it was losing approximately 15 per cent of its pilots *every month* from June through October.

The German success in thwarting the daylight offensive in the autumn of 1943 was, however, only a temporary result. Even as the Luftwaffe was inflicting heavy casualties on the Eighth's force structure, the American bomber force was swelling. It had numbered only 340 bombers in May 1943; by November its numbers had reached 902. But the results had been disappointing. At the end of the year General Hap Arnold shuffled his air commanders. Eaker moved to the Mediterranean, while General Carl Spaatz, overall commander of US Army Air Forces in Europe, brought Doolittle from the Mediterranean to replace Eaker. Part of the explanation for command changes had to

The finest of all American wartime fighters, the North American P-51 Mustang was developed to an RAF specification and entered service with the RAF before the USAAF. Later versions, such as this P-51D of the 66th Fighter Wing, powered by Rolls-Royce/Packard Merlin engines, were used as bomber escorts. Equipped with drop tanks in 1944, it was able to accompany B-17s and B-24s to Berlin and beyond.

do with Dwight Eisenhower's familiarity with Doolittle; it also had to do with the fact that he had achieved more impressive results than Eaker, particularly in regards to the use of tactical air power.

The new team enjoyed three important advantages over the situation in 1943: first, the Eighth's numbers and supply pipeline allowed for substantially heavier attrition; second, the Fifteenth Air Force flying out of the airfields around Foggia in Italy could attack targets in the Balkans as well as in southern Germany and Austria, thus confronting the Luftwaffe with an additional threat. But the most important change had to do with the new P-51; that aircraft was the best USAAF piston-engine fighter of the war and by March 1944 possessed sufficient range with drop tanks to reach Berlin itself. It was not available in sufficient numbers to take over all the escorting duties, but it could meet up with the B-17 and B-24 bomber formations at the outer reach of the P-47s, now also possessing greater range, and provide cover for the rest of the trip.

After a prolonged period of bad weather that lasted until late February 1944, the weather cleared for a week and the Eighth launched a series of devastating raids on the aircraft factories that produced Germany's fighters. Nevertheless, by a series of desperate measures, including shutting down bomber production, the Germans actually increased fighter production, but they came nowhere near to their targets for the year. The real success of the American attacks lay in the fact that the German fighter force came up to defend its production base and got blasted out of the sky by the P-47s and P-51s. In the period from February through May 1944, the Luftwaffe lost over 20 per cent of its fighter pilots every month. From January through May the Luftwaffe averaged 2,283 fighter pilots present for duty each month; it lost 2,262 pilots over the same period.

By May the Luftwaffe's fighter pilot force averaged three weeks of combat service after a training programme that provided minimal exposure to their combat aircraft (twenty-five hours in operational training squadrons). In fact, many could barely take off and land their aircraft; by this point in the war the Luftwaffe was running a heavy accident rate; and it was destroying almost as many of its aircraft by its own efforts as the Allies were shooting down. The effectiveness of German fighter pilots is suggested by Chuck Yeager's success in

Camera gun footage from a USAAF P-47 Thunderbolt showing the destruction of a Luftwaffe Focke-Wulf Fw 190 after a low-level dogfight over Germany in 1945.

destroying five German aircraft in a single engagement in October 1944. The first two crashed into each other as Yeager attacked them from the rear; the next two he shot down with his guns; and the fifth he chased into the ground. In May 1944 the Luftwaffe collapsed and from this point on in the war offered only sporadic opposition to Allied bombing attacks; American bomber losses also underwent a significant decline. The results of this fierce air battle were to give Allied air forces general air superiority over the European continent; Overlord, the Allied invasion of Normandy, would take place with minimal interference from the Luftwaffe.

By 1944 the Luftwaffe had evolved into two distinct forces. On one hand, there was a decreasing band of fighter pilots who had racked up incredible scores since the war's beginning. In effect, they had gained so much experience by constant active service that they were virtually unbeatable. (Unlike the Americans and British, who took their aces out of combat when they began to achieve significant totals and sent them back to train the next generation of fighter pilots.) The great mass of Luftwaffe fighter pilots, however, had no chance – with half the flying hours and one fifth of the hours in operational aircraft of their opponents.

On 1 April 1944 the bomber commands in England came under Eisenhower's control temporarily to prepare the way for the invasion. The bomber barons complained about being subordinated to the needs of a land operation, but in fact they had no political choice, given the importance of Overlord in Allied strategy. Moreover, in the face of the devastating losses in the battle of Berlin, Harris had no military choice. Tedder, Eisenhower's deputy, devised a plan for using Allied air power to cut off the invasion area from reinforcements by destroying the railroad and road networks of northern France. Harris, playing on Churchill's fears about post-war Anglo-French relations, argued that Bomber Command could not hit precision targets such as marshalling yards without substantial collateral damage. He was wrong; with the new techniques and within range of navigational aids in England,

B-17G Flying Forts of the 303rd Bomb Group, known as the 'Hells Angels', drop strings of 440-pound incendiary cluster bombs and smoke markers during a daylight raid on German factories in the Ruhr in 1944.

Bomber Command was able to inflict terrible damage on French transportation networks. American strategic bombers and tactical air forces also contributed to an immensely successful campaign.

By early June, French railroads were at a standstill and most of the bridges in the road system had been destroyed by Allied air power. The SS division *Das Reich* left Limoges on 11 June and did not get to Normandy until the end of the month. Only the barge traffic down the Seine (which, by an oversight, Allied air power failed to attack) provided enough supplies to keep the battle going in Normandy until early August, when the entire front collapsed. The Allied advance after the breakout came to a halt on the German frontier and thereafter remained nearly stationary for the next six months – largely due to the supply difficulties the Allies now confronted in crossing the devastated French roads and railroads they had themselves destroyed.

By the spring of 1944 the Anglo-American forces possessed so much air power that Eisenhower could allow Spaatz and Doolittle to begin a major campaign against German synthetic oil factories in the Reich. In early April the Fifteenth Air Force began a sustained bombing of the Romanian oil wells at Ploesti from Italy. In mid May Spaatz and

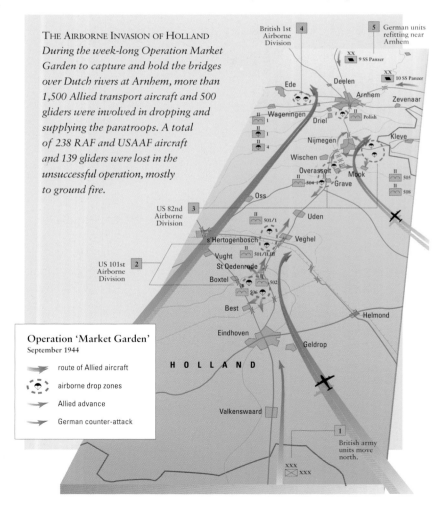

THE AIRBORNE INVASION OF HOLLAND
During the week-long Operation Market Garden to capture and hold the bridges over Dutch rivers at Arnhem, more than 1,500 Allied transport aircraft and 500 gliders were involved in dropping and supplying the paratroops. A total of 238 RAF and USAAF aircraft and 139 gliders were lost in the unsuccessful operation, mostly to ground fire.

British 1st Airborne Division **4**

5 German units refitting near Arnhem

XX 9 SS Panzer

XX 10 SS Panzer

Ede
Deelen
Arnhem
Zevenaar

Wageningen
Driel
Polish

Kleve

Nijmegen
Wischen

Overasselt
Mook
Grave

505

508

Oss

US 82nd Airborne Division **3**

501/1
Uden

s'Hertogenbosch
Veghel

US 101st Airborne Division **2**

Vught
St Oedenrode
501/II,III

Boxtel
502
506

Best

Helmond

Eindhoven
Geldrop

H O L L A N D

Valkenswaard

Operation 'Market Garden'
September 1944

route of Allied aircraft

airborne drop zones

Allied advance

German counter-attack

1
British army units move north.

XXX XXX

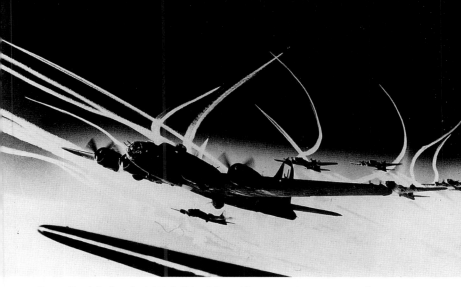

Contrails of the bomber's 'Little Friends' provide a protective cover over a formation of 390th Bomb Group B-17F Flying Forts on their way to bomb targets deep in Germany.

Doolittle began air attacks on the synthetic oil industry in the Reich which supplied the bulk of the Wehrmacht's fuels. The combination of these resulted in a general collapse of Germany's sources of petroleum and petroleum products by early summer. The direct as well as the indirect effects were devastating. German ground forces, already restricted in mobility by Allied air forces in the east as well as the west, now found themselves with almost no gasoline for movement. The Ardennes offensive, launched in December 1944 against the Americans, lacked sufficient fuel to reach its operational objectives; German planning rested on the assumption that attacking forces would capture the fuel they needed. But equally serious for the Germans was the fact that the collapse of petroleum production meant that there was insufficient fuel for training new pilots or tank crews to reasonable standards.

A series of devastating Allied ground offensives from east and west marked the last five months of the war. German soldiers fought in all theatres without aid from the Luftwaffe. Meanwhile, great formations of four-engined bombers battered German cities and targets by day and

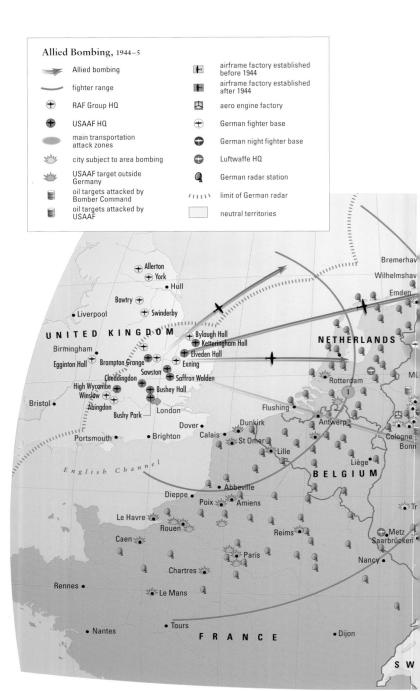

Allied Bombing, 1944–5

- ➤ Allied bombing
- ─ fighter range
- ⊕ RAF Group HQ
- ⊕ USAAF HQ
- ⬭ main transportation attack zones
- ☼ city subject to area bombing
- ☼ USAAF target outside Germany
- 🛢 oil targets attacked by Bomber Command
- 🛢 oil targets attacked by USAAF

- ⊞ airframe factory established before 1944
- ⊞ airframe factory established after 1944
- ⬟ aero engine factory
- ⊕ German fighter base
- ⬤ German night fighter base
- ⬤ Luftwaffe HQ
- ◖ German radar station
- ⸗⸗ limit of German radar
- ☐ neutral territories

Bremerhav
Wilhelmshav
Emden

Allerton
York
Hull
Bawtry
Swinderby
Liverpool

UNITED KINGDOM
Bylaugh Hall
Ketteringham Hall
Elveden Hall
NETHERLANDS
Birmingham
Exning
Egginton Hall
Brampton Grange
Sawston
Saffron Walden
Cheddingdon
Rotterdam
High Wycombe
Bushey Hall
Winslow
Bushey Hall
Flushing
Antwerp
Cologne
Bristol
Abingdon
Bushy Park
London
Bonn
Dover
Dunkirk
Calais
St Omer
Liège
Portsmouth
Brighton
Lille
BELGIUM
English Channel
Abbeville
Dieppe
Poix
Amiens
Le Havre
Rouen
Reims
Tr
Caen
Metz
Saarbrücken
Paris
Nancy
Chartres
Rennes
Le Mans
Nantes
Tours
FRANCE
Dijon
Mu
S W

OPERATION POINT BLANK

The combined Allied bomber offensive against Germany, code-named Point Blank,
resulted from the Casablanca Conference held in January 1943, which directed that
the US Eighth Air Force was to bomb by day, while RAF Bomber Command carry
out night bombing. The heaviest Point Blank raid of the war occurred on 14 October
1944 when more than 3,000 Allied bombers took part in Operation Hurricane
against Cologne, Duisburg and Brunswick.

1 May 1943: Spitfire, range 175 miles

2 August 1943: P.47 with drop tank,
range 375 miles

3 March 1944: P.51 with drop tank,
range 600 miles

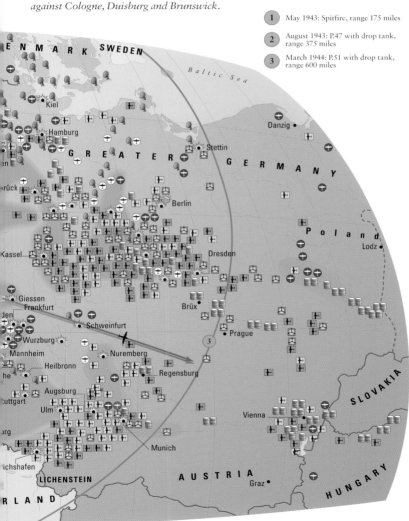

With a top speed of nearly 430 mph, the long-nose Focke-Wulf Fw 190D-9 Dora was produced to combat the around-the-clock Allied bombing armadas that pulverized Germany after D-Day. The example illustrated belongs to JG 26 and wears 'Defence of the Reich' stripes on the rear fuselage.

night. The Americans continued their attacks on the synthetic oil industry as the Germans made desperate efforts to rebuild shattered plants – but all for nought, as the Americans, informed as to how the Germans were progressing by Ultra, wrecked the repair efforts again and again. Harris and Bomber Command returned to attacking the Reich's cities; with German early-warning sites on the French coast in Allied hands, and plagued by fuel shortages, Luftwaffe night fighters could no longer provide the opposition that had devastated Bomber Command in its raid on Nuremberg in March.

Both strategic bombing forces supported Tedder's new plan to attack Germany's transportation industry. These attacks, which began in September, caused a creeping paralysis in the entire German war economy and its ability to support the Wehrmacht. The result was a general collapse, east and west, in the spring of 1945 as the Wehrmacht, lacking fuel and ammunition, could no longer fulfil the Führer's promise to stage a final *Götterdämmerung* on the ruins of the Reich. The collapse of the German transportation system undoubtedly shortened the war by a number of months and prevented really effective resistance from occurring once the Allies had breached the Rhine.

Air Power and the Winning of the War

The interwar apostles of air power had argued that the aeroplane would be the decisive weapon of the next war. According to theory, if the nations employed their aircraft properly, that is to say in great strategic bombing fleets, they would bring victory swiftly and without the cost that had accompanied victory in the First World War. Yet, strategic bombing replicated the attrition of the previous war, except that attrition came now in terms of aircraft and aircrews rather than mud-stained infantry. Month after month, year after year, crews climbed into their bombers to fly over the European continent, while their generals came to measure success by drops in percentage points of bombers and fighters lost rather than in terms of yards gained. As Anthony Verrier pointed out in *The Bomber Offensive*:

> The laws of war applied as much to the strategic air offensive waged over Europe's skies through five-and-a-half bitter years as they did to the sailors and soldiers on the distant seas or in the sand and mud below. Occasionally, the airman may have felt himself living and fighting in a new dimension, just as the air force commander may have sometimes felt he enjoyed a freedom of manoeuvre denied to admirals and generals. But the airman died, and the air force commander was defeated, unless the laws were kept. When they were kept, success came; until they could be kept, hope was kept alive by courage alone.

There was no cheap and easy way to victory through air power.

Again in contradiction to the pre-war theories, air power proved crucial in winning the war because of the very breadth of its contribution. Without long-range aircraft, the Allied navies might not have won the battle of the Atlantic as soon as they did; from that achievement flowed the possibility of projecting Anglo-American air power and ground forces on to the European continent in 1944. The strategic bombing campaign made possible the achievement of air superiority over the continent as a result of the great air battles lasting from January through May 1944. With that air superiority the western powers achieved a successful lodgement in Normandy and impeded

American B-24 Liberator bombers being mass produced on the production line at a new Consolidated plant at Fort Worth, Texas in 1943. More than 19,000 B-24s were manufactured during the war, and a number of these impressive aircraft were still in service in 1952.

German supplies from reaching the battlefront. Equally important, Allied tactical air forces and the close air support they provided contributed significantly to making some of the tactical weaknesses of Allied ground forces.

But the most controversial aspect of Anglo-American air power had to do with the Combined Bomber Offensive, the strategic bombing effort against Germany. This author at least would rate its contribution as one of the four essential elements in Allied victory over Nazi Germany, the others being the Eastern Front, the battle of the Atlantic and American productive superiority. Let us then consider some of the particular contributions that the bombing efforts made to winning the war.

It is hard to measure the impact of bombing because, in contradiction to many of the tenets of air power, so much of its effect was indirect. We can, of course, measure increases in German production due to Speer's utilization of the whole of Europe's economic structure. But what would German-controlled industry have produced, had the Reich's cities not been pounded by British bombers? Perhaps the best that we can say is that German utilization of their own economic resources and those of the European nations under their control was severely impeded by the increasingly effective bombing after 1942. Moreover, the quality of German-produced weapons declined significantly after 1942.

The responses that the Nazi government made to the night-bomber offensive suggest the profound indirect impact of the Combined Bomber Offensive. The growth of the Flak (anti-aircraft fire) forces defending the Reich at a time when on any number of fronts German ground forces were confronting increasingly numerous and effective opponents suggests the impact the bombing made on the minds of the Nazi leadership and their worries that the home front might again collapse as in 1918. The number of Flak batteries rose from 791 guarding the Reich in 1940, to 967 in 1941, 1,148 in 1942 and 2,132 in 1943. By the end of 1943 the Germans had nearly 10,000 high-velocity anti-aircraft guns and 500,000 men firing huge numbers of shells into the skies over the Reich and hitting little. The impact of such weapons and manpower on other fronts in 1943 or 1944 hardly needs emphasis.

The second indirect effect of 'area' bombing also occurred in the minds of the Nazi leadership. Worried by the bombing's impact on German morale, Hitler and his advisers hit on a strategy of retaliation, one entirely in accord with the tenets of Douhet and Trenchard. As a result, the Germans poured enormous resources into the so-called revenge weapons, the V-1 and V-2. The former did not require a huge investment, but the latter made no sense at all. The V-2 demanded complex technological support; it was inordinately expensive; it used up scarce resources; and its production overloaded the instrument and electrical-component industries. With such heavy emphasis on 'revenge weapons' the Nazi leaders continued short-changing the air defence forces. After the war the US Strategic Bombing Survey estimated that the industrial effort and resources devoted to these weapons was roughly equivalent to that of the production of 24,000 fighter aircraft. A more recent analysis has calculated that the V-2 programme was roughly equivalent in proportional terms to the cost of the Manhattan project (the atomic bomb) in the United States – all in order to produce a one-way weapon that carried a ton of explosives and needed a target the size of the entire metropolitan area of London.

The American effort is easier to evaluate. In 1943 the campaign's results were disappointing, especially considering its losses. But it did impose heavy losses on the Luftwaffe and these carried over into 1944. In that year the massive campaign by the Eighth Air Force against the Luftwaffe's production base slowed the rate of increase in German aircraft production. But its most important contribution was the fact that it pulled the Luftwaffe's fighter force up into the air, where US long-range fighters could destroy it. The collapse in May 1944 was the direct result. The attacks on the German and Romanian oil industries made the regeneration of the Luftwaffe's fighting strength impossible; it also presented the Germans with insoluble problems in the ground war. In February 1945 Soviet armies conquered the province of Silesia in less than a week; German forces in the area possessed over 1,000 tanks, but all were immobilized by lack of fuel and were consequently useless.

Strategic air power also contributed to the campaign in Normandy and the eventual collapse of Nazi Germany in the spring of 1945. Tedder's transportation plan worked particularly well due to the capabilities Bomber Command developed in its efforts over the Reich. The tragedy was that having developed capabilities that allowed it to bomb even more accurately than the Eighth and Fifteenth Air Forces, Bomber Command's leadership returned to a policy of city-busting that minimized rather than maximized the possibilities.

In the end, air power did not win the war in Europe by itself. Rather its contribution reflected a broad-based application of capabilities that contributed significantly to victory in the air, on land and at sea. The failures of the Luftwaffe were symbolic of the Third Reich's fate. The German leaders held goals that were manifestly beyond the reach of their nation. The devastating effect of German successes in the first war years should not disguise the dilettantism of those who conducted the Reich's grand strategy. Intermixed with an exceedingly high level of competence on the tactical and operational levels was a general inability to see the relationship between ends and means. The Germans waged the struggle with operational and tactical competence to the bitter end, but the tenacity of that defence only ensured that the final defeat would be all the more terrible.

The scene of devastation seen at Nuremberg in 1945 was the result of four years of constant Allied bombing which began on the night of 12/13 October 1941 by Bomber Command Stirlings, and ended with daylight raids by Eighth Air Force B-17s in 1945.

CHAPTER FOUR

Air War in the Pacific

A view of an American task force of carriers and battleships, across a flight deck packed full of F4U Corsairs at the end of the Pacific war. In July 1945, fourteen US carriers of Task Force 38 were joined by four British carriers to attack naval bases, airfields and military installations on the Japanese home islands.

Air War in the Pacific

MOST HISTORIES OF THE Second World War, with their Eurocentric emphases, begin on 1 September 1939 and date the entrance of the United States and Japan into the war on 7 December 1941 with the attack on Pearl Harbor. In fact, the Pacific war began in June 1937. In response to a Chinese boycott of Japanese goods and a series of incidents, the Japanese army launched a massive invasion of China. However, without realistic strategic or political conceptions, the Japanese soon found themselves sucked deeper and deeper into an interminable war.

The China 'Incident' provided Japanese air forces with considerable combat experience at relatively little cost. While Chinese ground forces, particularly early in the conflict, put up reasonable resistance, Chinese air capabilities were virtually non-existent. As in the Second World

The Mitsubishi G3M was the Imperial Japanese army's standard medium bomber when Japan entered the Second World War, and three days after Pearl Harbor, the type, code-named 'Nell' took part in the sinking of the British battleship HMS Prince of Wales *and battle-cruiser HMS* Repulse *off Malaya.*

War, the Japanese showed a level of ruthlessness and callousness towards civilian casualties that the Germans would soon emulate. At Nanking Japanese aircraft bombed a defenceless city; massed rapes and murders by the army followed. But the war with China, no matter how successful, steadily increased tension with the western powers, while the explosion of war in Europe offered the Japanese navy, which had long based its budget on an expansion of Japanese interests into Southeast Asia, considerable opportunities. The collapse of France in June 1940 obviously increased those opportunities; in July the Japanese demanded, and after a short military action obtained, the right to establish bases in the northern half of French Indo-china; a beleaguered Britain and an uncertain United States stood aside. The Japanese aimed more at closing China off from its sources of supply than at moving against the possessions of the European powers.

The next year the Japanese repeated their actions – this time demanding the French yield bases in southern Indo-china. There could be no mistaking the intent: occupation of such bases could only mean the Japanese were aiming at the projection of their power against Malaya and the Dutch East Indies. The American response was decisive, perhaps too decisive; the US government froze Japanese assets in the United States and embargoed all strategic goods, including petroleum products. Oil was not supposed to be on the list, but was mistakenly included. Once on the list, it could not be removed. That inclusion made the Pacific war inevitable in the immediate future, because without access to petroleum, the Japanese military would run out of fuel within a year.

Japanese thinking about a Pacific war had focused on a defensive war in which submarines and aircraft, based in the central Pacific, would damage the US fleet as it moved across the Pacific and thus create sufficiently favourable odds for their main fleet to win a crushing, decisive victory off the home islands. But the creation of a carrier strike force in April 1941, with six large carriers, offered riskier but more enticing prospects. Moreover, despite a virtually non-existent system of interservice co-operation, the Japanese determined to attack Malaya, the Dutch East Indies and the Philippines all at the same time. But such an offensive would leave an open flank at which the US fleet could strike.

Beginning in late summer the commander of the Combined Fleet, Admiral Isoroku Yamamoto – a man with few illusions about Japanese prospects against the United States – pushed through a plan to send the First Air Fleet with its six carriers against Pearl Harbor to destroy the US fleet at the outbreak of war. In retrospect, Yamamoto's plan represented a terrible mistake; yet at the time it seemed to make operational and strategic sense. If successful, it would remove the US fleet from the military equation and, given the strong isolationist and anti-war currents in the United States, one might expect that the Americans would react as the Russians had to the surprise attack on Port Arthur in 1904. What is astonishing is the level of risk that Yamamoto ran, both in launching a vast raid across the northern

An Imperial Japanese Navy A6M2 Zero fighter carrying a long-range drop tank takes off from the carrier Akagi *on 7 December 1941 to escort Kate torpedo-bombers and Val dive-bombers during their attack on Pearl Harbor.*

Pacific and in basing his entire plan on the untested capabilities of carrier-borne strike aircraft.

Japan had only 2,800 combat aircraft – 1,300 navy and 1,500 army – to execute its ambitious plans to cripple the American Pacific Fleet and conquer the economic resources of South-east Asia. The Japanese pilots themselves were experienced and all were graduates of the toughest pilot-training programme of any nation in the world. Japanese aircraft, especially the Zero fighter, were far superior to those of their opponents – a nasty surprise to Allied pilots when their intelligence had led them to believe the Japanese were flying obsolete aircraft. Moreover, Japanese naval forces and their weapons, especially the long-lance torpedo, were distinctly superior to anything their enemies possessed. Nevertheless, while US combat aircraft were inferior in 1941 and 1942, all the Americans had to do was to hold the line and wait for the new, more modern aircraft and ships that would be arriving from the United States once production hit its stride.

JAPAN *ÜBER ALLES*

As diplomatic negotiations unravelled, Japanese carriers crossed the northern Pacific, while other Japanese forces gathered in the western Pacific to undertake operations against the Philippines and Malaya. The Americans recognized the signs; they were already deciphering a significant number of Japanese diplomatic codes, but however much they recognized war's inevitability, they failed to recognize that it was going to happen *on that particular day* – 7 December 1941. Radar operators picked up the mass of Japanese aircraft approaching from the north, but the officer on duty at the air defence centre informed them that it was only an expected flight of B-17s coming in from the States. At Pearl Harbor, seven battleships lay moored off Ford Island, another one in the nearby dry dock; two carriers were away delivering aircraft to Midway and Wake Islands, while one was on the west coast – the one piece of luck that occurred for the Allies in the first six months of the Pacific war.

Japanese torpedo aircraft and dive-bombers inflicted severe damage on the warships in Pearl. Of the battleships only the *Pennsylvania* escaped relatively unscathed, ironically in dry dock, although the two destroyers in front of her were seriously damaged. Despite this seeming success, the Japanese suffered a serious political and strategic defeat by

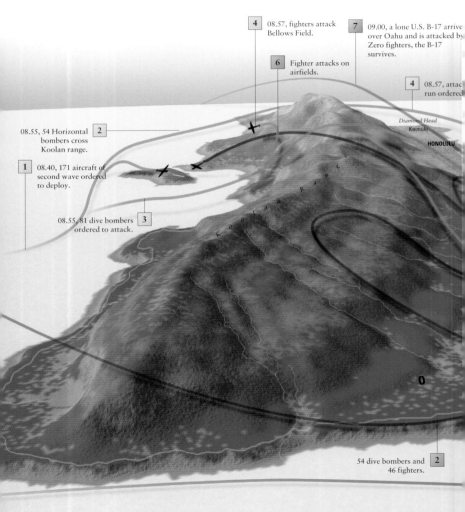

4 08.57, fighters attack Bellows Field.

7 09.00, a lone U.S. B-17 arrives over Oahu and is attacked by Zero fighters, the B-17 survives.

6 Fighter attacks on airfields.

4 08.57, attack run ordered

Diamond Head
Kaimuki
HONOLULU

2 08.55, 54 Horizontal bombers cross Koolan range.

1 08.40, 171 aircraft of second wave ordered to deploy.

3 08.55, 81 dive bombers ordered to attack.

Koolau Range

2 54 dive bombers and 46 fighters.

Pacific Ocean

DAY OF INFAMY

On 7 December 1941, 465 Imperial Japanese Navy aircraft launched from six carriers in the Northern Pacific to attack US Pacific Fleet warships at Pearl Harbor, Hawaii. Although eighteen US ships were sunk or badly damaged, including eight battleships, none of the Pacific Fleet's three carriers, USS Lexington, Enterprise or Saratoga were in port during the attack.

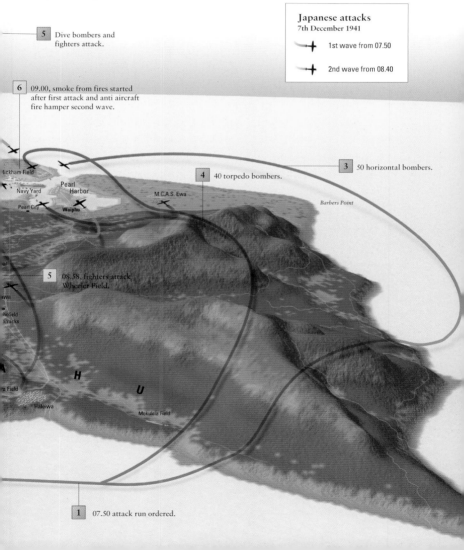

Japanese attacks
7th December 1941

1st wave from 07.50

2nd wave from 08.40

5 Dive bombers and fighters attack.

6 09.00, smoke from fires started after first attack and anti aircraft fire hamper second wave.

Hickham Field

Navy Yard   Pearl Harbor

Pearl City   Waiphu

M.C.A.S. Ewa

Barbers Point

3 50 horizontal bombers.

4 40 torpedo bombers.

5 08.58, fighters attack Wheeler Field.

Schofield Barracks

Field

H   U

Haleiwa   Mokuleia Field

1 07.50 attack run ordered.

their attack on Pearl Harbor, for the attack unified the United States as nothing else could have done. But Pearl Harbor was also an operational failure, for by not attacking the great petroleum tank farms that contained well over 1,000,000 tons of fuel, the Japanese allowed the US Navy to operate from Pearl Harbor in 1942 and early 1943 – as it could not have done if the fuel had been destroyed.

The Japanese took full advantage of their success at Pearl to smash the European empires in South-east Asia. In the Philippines, eight hours after the attack on Pearl, attacking Japanese aircraft caught the resident American B-17s parked wing-tip to wing-tip and destroyed most of them. With US air power in the Philippines destroyed, the Japanese landed unopposed, against light opposition. They rapidly advanced against defences made more vulnerable by General Douglas MacArthur's incompetence in attempting to defend the whole main island instead of retreating immediately to Bataan as the original plans called for. Off Malaya, Japanese aircraft caught the British battleship *Prince of Wales* and battle cruiser *Repulse* attempting to prevent amphibious landings in northern Malaya. Admiral Tom Phillips, commander of the force, had been a firm advocate of the invulnerability of capital ships against aircraft; he paid for his belief with his life and with the destruction of his ships.

Over the next five months the Japanese swept all before them: Malaya, Singapore, the Philippines, Guam, the Dutch East Indies and Burma. Where Japanese and Allied fleets met, the Japanese emerged with hardly a scratch, while Japanese aircraft covered the movement of amphibious operations and attacked enemy installations. At a cost of less than a dozen warships and barely 100 aircraft, the Japanese conquered South-east Asia. The problem for the Japanese, however, was how to hold the vast conquests against an aroused and furious American polity. Exacerbating their strategic difficulties were two factors: first, the occurrence of 'victory' disease in an even more virulent form than that which Nazi leaders suffered in June 1940; and second, the lack of any clear military objective beyond that of holding their island barrier in the central Pacific. In late January 1942 US carriers raided the Marshalls and Gilberts; the attacks were meant to distract the Japanese from operations in South-east Asia, but they failed to achieve that object or to inflict serious damage. In March a two-carrier task force, the carriers *Yorktown* and *Lexington*, attacked Japanese landing forces off eastern New Guinea and were more successful. American torpedo bombers discovered that their torpedoes were no more effective than those used by their submarines, but dive-bombers sank four ships and damaged nine others (including two destroyers and a light cruiser). The attack convinced the Japanese that they needed carrier support to complete the conquest of New Guinea; two large carriers moved to the area for an operation in late April.

The Japanese military leaders were already debating the next major move. Some within the navy wanted to strike at Australia, a move the army, considering the distances and logistical difficulties, rejected. Others in the navy suggested a strike into the Indian Ocean to link up with the Germans; that option too found little favour with the army. Both army and navy looked at Hawaii and decided that the American naval and air bases were probably too well defended. With no clear decision, the navy sent five fast carriers into the Indian Ocean, where they chased the British fleet back to Kenya, sank the old carrier, *Hermes*, and two cruisers, launched heavy raids against Ceylon and sank over 100,000 tons of shipping. In retrospect the Japanese might have stayed in the Indian Ocean and caused irreparable damage to the Allied cause by cutting off British forces in the Middle East from their logistical support. But since there was never a co-ordinated strategy among the Axis powers and since the Japanese army refused to change its strategic focus on the Soviet Union and China, the fleet returned.

Meanwhile, the Americans had been preparing a daring raid, using Army Air Force B-25s. The medium bombers would fly off the new aircraft carrier *Hornet* to attack Tokyo from a distance greater than carrier aircraft could reach and would then continue on to land in

Despite its fixed undercarriage and dated appearance, the Aichi D3A21 carrier-based dive-bomber was highly manoeuvrable and was no easy prey for US fighters. After Pearl Harbor, the 'Val' was responsible for sinking the British carrier HMS Hermes, *and the cruisers HMS* Cornwall *and* Dorsetshire *in April 1942.*

China. Because of Japanese picket ships in the central Pacific, the Americans had to launch early and attack the home islands during the day. The B-25s took Japanese defences by surprise. While they inflicted relatively minor damage on Tokyo, the shock of the attack resulted in a strategic decision of immense consequence: the Japanese navy would launch a massive attack on Midway, to be followed up by a landing force to seize the island. Thus, two major Japanese strategic decisions resulted from the American carrier strikes. The first was already in motion as the Americans struck Tokyo; it involved the movement of two Japanese carriers to support amphibious operations designed to take Port Moresby and place the whole of New Guinea in Japanese hands.

By late April 1942, the breaking of the Japanese navy's most widely used operational code allowed American naval intelligence to predict that the Japanese were about to strike Port Moresby. Magic – code name for this intelligence – also alerted the Americans of Japanese intentions to attack Midway. Admiral Chester Nimitz, commander of the navy in the Pacific, ordered the carrier *Lexington* south to reinforce the *Yorktown*. The resulting battle of the Coral Sea was the first battle in naval history where the fleets never saw each other; carrier aircraft inflicted all the damage. The battle itself involved much confusion. US naval aircraft sank the small carrier *Shoho*, while Japanese land-based aircraft from Rabaul attacked a task force of Allied surface ships coming from Australia, which was also bombed by B-17s (all of which missed). Japanese carrier bombers were then ambushed by fighters guided by the *Lexington*'s radar; in darkness and bad weather some Japanese planes actually attempted to land on the US carriers and were shot down.

On the next day the opposing carriers finally found each other. American dive-bombers damaged the large carrier *Shokaku* substantially, but missed the *Zuikaku* entirely. The Japanese hit the *Yorktown* with a bomb that did light damage, but got two torpedoes and a bomb into the *Lexington*. Nevertheless, within a short period the great carrier was steaming at twenty-five knots and conducting flight operations. However, after temporary repairs, a tremendous explosion caused by gasoline fumes shook the *Lexington*; two hours later another large explosion caused fires to rage out of control, and the captain ordered the crew to abandon ship. Thus ended the inconclusive battle

The first of sixteen B-25B Mitchell medium bombers of the Seventeenth AAF led by Lt. Col. J. H. Doolittle lifts off from the flight deck of the carrier USS Hornet *on 18 April 1942, 668 miles from Tokyo, for the first USAAF bombing raid on Japanese soil.*

of the Coral Sea. In terms of tonnage sunk the Japanese were the winners. But, as with Jutland, the tonnage figures were misleading; both *Shokaku* and *Zuikaku* were out of action for the Midway operation – the former because of battle damage, the latter because of aircraft losses. The Japanese also abandoned their attempt to take Port Moresby by amphibious assault. Instead they decided to build fighter and seaplane bases at Guadalcanal and Tulagi to support a further assault on Port Moresby.

Meanwhile, the *Yorktown* rushed back to Pearl, where she arrived on 22 May. Engineers indicated that ninety days was a reasonable time for repairing the damage. Nimitz suggested three and they compromised on seven. On the 29th *Yorktown* headed north-west to join the carriers *Hornet* and *Enterprise*: land-based aircraft were to find the enemy carriers, which carrier strikes would then hit.

Having decided to take Midway Island, Admiral Yamamoto, commander of the Combined Fleet, designed a complicated operation to divert the Americans from his intentions. Light carriers would strike Dutch Harbor and US bases in Alaska. Then the main carrier force, now only four large carriers, would eliminate US air units on Midway and suppress the defenders. Finally, the main battle fleet would arrive to combine with the fast carriers and eliminate the US Navy in a Mahanian 'decisive' battle. But, alerted by Magic intercepts, the Americans had eyes only for the coming attack on Midway.

On the morning of 4 June the Japanese carriers were within range of Midway. Float planes from accompanying cruisers and battleships flew off to search out any US naval vessels, but Japan's run of luck, which had been extraordinary thus far, was about to run out. The floatplane scheduled for the quadrant where the US carriers were located developed engine trouble and set off late. The first attack on Midway went in and was returning when the Japanese received word of the possible presence of an American carrier. Already under attack from land-based marine aircraft and army B-17s, they brought back the Midway strike planes in order to prepare for another attack.

At this point – with the Japanese decks covered with aircraft armed with torpedoes and armour-piercing bombs, refueling hoses and gasoline bowsers to refuel the returning Midway strike and ground-attack weapons for a second strike on Midway – the American torpedo bombers attacked. Japanese fighters slaughtered the attackers, but three waves of torpedo bombers forced the Zeros down to deck level, while anti-aircraft guns on the covering ships were depressed to the maximum. At that critical moment, the American dive-bombers arrived. Two bombs hit the *Akagi* and detonated aircraft, bombs and torpedoes in an instant funeral pyre; the *Kaga* received four hits, one of which destroyed its bridge and superstructure, while the *Soryu* was hit with three bombs. Within minutes half of the Japanese navy's fast carriers were blazing wrecks. The one survivor, the *Hiryu*, got off two strikes at the *Yorktown* that put three bombs and two torpedoes into the American carrier. Three hours later US carrier dive-bombers got the *Hiryu*. With four of his best carriers lost, Yamamoto conceded defeat; the Americans had won a major victory and irrevocably reversed the Japanese tide.

Slightly damaged in the Coral Sea, the carrier USS Yorktown *suffered heavy damage from Japanese dive-bombers and torpedo bombers during the battle of Midway that eventually led to her sinking on 4 June 1942.*

THE BATTLE OF ATTRITION: THE SOLOMONS AND NEW GUINEA

The American victory at Midway improved the Allied position on the defensive side of the ledger. But for taking offensive action, the Americans had scanty reserves – not until 1943 would they reap advantage from the productive capabilities of their industry. Nevertheless, Japanese pressure reaching down to the Solomon Islands threatened to cut communication lines between the United States and Australia. In particular, the Japanese had almost completed an airfield on Guadalcanal that would dominate the southern Solomons and threaten the New Hebrides.

Aware of the risks, Admiral Ernest J. King, commander-in-chief of the US fleet and Admiral Nimitz committed the 1st Marine Division to capturing Guadalcanal and its almost completed airstrip in order to block further Japanese encroachments. Luckily for the Americans, Japanese overconfidence led them to commit only construction crews to the building of the airfield. Consequently, the marines overran the construction site with little opposition and completed the airfield, soon named Henderson Field, in a few days. However, at sea, Vice-Admiral Frank Fletcher, commanding the naval forces, abandoned the marines, while that night the cruisers guarding the landings suffered a catastrophe at the hands of a Japanese cruiser force at the battle of Savo Island (four out of five sunk), a grim warning of how far the US surface navy had to go.

But the crucial piece in the puzzle was the marine hold over Henderson Field – that and continuing Japanese overconfidence. An operating airfield on Guadalcanal would allow the Americans to dominate the seas around the Solomons during daylight and severely impede Japanese efforts to regain their position. One week after the landing, US destroyers brought in bombs, ammunition and fuel; five days later nineteen fighters and twelve dive-bombers arrived to provide the Americans with a slim but significant margin of aerial superiority over the Solomons. The landings on Guadalcanal represented the opening chapter in a long and bloody contest that saw both sides make

A Douglas SBD-3 Dauntless dive-bomber from the carrier USS Enterprise flies near bombed Japanese ships at Guadalcanal during the American's seizure of the island in February 1943, the air superiority gained with the capture of Henderson Field provided the margin of victory.

increasingly large commitments. Because the Japanese air bases were so far away, American aircraft ruled the day throughout the central and southern Solomons. Yet, despite their advantages in radar, the Americans did not do well in night surface actions. But when the Japanese were caught in daylight, such as happened to the battleship *Hiei*, the results were usually fatal. What was called the 'slot' – two parallel lines of islands that form the Solomons chain – became one of the most contested areas of water in the world.

But the Japanese gave as good as they got. In late October the two navies again fought in a major carrier battle, the Japanese this time coming out ahead. The Americans lost the *Hornet*, and the *Enterprise* was damaged, and two Japanese carriers, the *Zuiho* and the *Shokaku*, were also damaged. The air losses were roughly equal – the Japanese losing nearly one hundred aircraft, the Americans seventy-four. US naval forces withdrew first, but harassing attacks from land-based aircraft then persuaded the Japanese admiral to pull out too. On 15 November US aircraft caught a major Japanese effort to supply their hard-pressed troops on Guadalcanal and sank six transports and one heavy cruiser.

By the next morning the Japanese were down to four transports, which they beached; some survivors, but little equipment or supplies, made it ashore; approximately six thousand Japanese soldiers died in the carnage.

Thus, Japanese forces on Guadalcanal, already diseased and close to starvation, now had even more mouths to feed. Further supply attempts were reduced to fast destroyers running down the slot at night with rafts to be launched at Japanese-controlled beaches. Then followed a desperate run back up the slot at flank speed in order to be out of range by daylight. In January 1943, for one of the few times in the war, the Japanese cut their losses and retreated, after losing 23,000 out of the 36,000 troops dispatched to drive the Americans off the island.

While marines, soldiers and sailors fought on Guadalcanal under the cover of land-based and sea-borne air power, MacArthur's Australian and US army troops were waging an equally bloody struggle of attrition against the Japanese in New Guinea. The conditions under which the ground forces fought were miserable, but again Allied air power played a decisive role in isolating Japanese forces from reinforcements and adequate resupply. Here too, the struggle had few decisive moments, but the cumulative impact of the attrition of skilled Japanese naval and army aircrews was decisive in the future outcome of the war. Japanese ace Saburo Sakai had arrived in the theatre in summer 1942 in a wing of eighty pilots. By early 1943 there were only eight survivors, including Saburo, who, blind in one eye and barely able to see out of the other, returned to Rabaul after an epic flight from Guadalcanal.

The putative aim of the New Guinea fighting in 1943 and 1944 was to reach the great Japanese base at Rabaul. While carrier air made substantial contributions to the advance, the Fifth Air Force with its land-based aircraft was even more important in gaining air superiority and isolating the battlefield. Its commander, Major-General George C. Kenney, proved one of the most adaptive and competent air commanders of the war. He also proved a tough advocate of both air power and of his command's interests before MacArthur's sycophantic

The A6M2 Zero flown by Imperial Japanese Navy ace Saburo Sakai of the Tainan Kokutai *based at Lae, New Guinea, in July 1942. Satai survived the war as the third highest scoring fighter pilot, with sixty-four confirmed victories in China and the Pacific.*

staff. On Kenney's introduction to the theatre, MacArthur's chief of staff, Brigadier-General Richard Sutherland, attempted to lecture him on how best to employ air power. Kenney grabbed a piece of paper off Sutherland's desk, put a dot in the centre with a pencil, and announced that the dot represented what the chief of staff knew about air power, while the surrounding sea of white represented what he (Kenney) knew.

General Hap Arnold had sent Kenney to the theatre in August 1942 to clean up a monumental mess in which a badly run command was making little contribution to winning the war, whilst wasting large amounts of resources. Kenney cleared the field by firing five generals and a host of colonels. The atmosphere in the Fifth Air Force became one of energy and determination; its air crews were now going to kill Japanese in large numbers. So far the Fifth Air Force had stolidly followed pre-war doctrine by bombing Japanese ships from a high altitude, where enemy flak rarely reached. The results were spectacular water spouts, huge numbers of dead fish and little damage to the Japanese. Kenney immediately decreed that even the B-17s would bomb from lower altitudes. He modified his B-25 medium bombers to carry eight machine-guns in their nose and began an intensive programme to retrain aircrews to attack from low altitude by 'skipping' their bombs directly into enemy ships.

As a retrained and refocused force, Kenney's aircraft and crews made a decisive showing in the battle of the Bismarck Sea. The

The Grumman F6F Hellcat was the most successful ship-based fighter of the Second World War. The Hellcat, which first entered service with VF-9 on the carrier USS Essex in August 1943, was credited with no fewer than 4,947 of the 6,477 enemy aircraft claimed by US Navy carrier pilots.

Japanese were involved in a major reinforcement to move their 51st Division from Rabaul to New Guinea. Eight transports, supported by eight destroyers, with a hundred aircraft flying cover, moved along the New Britain coast out into the Solomon Sea. Alerted by Magic intercepts, Kenney and the Fifth Air Force were ready. Initial attacks by B-17s got two transports, and as Japanese ships moved through the Dampier Strait, their lookouts caught sight of nearly a hundred Allied aircraft headed at full speed and at very low level straight toward them. B-25s, A-20s and Australian Beaufighters slashed into the Japanese convoy. By the evening Allied aircraft had sunk the transports and half the destroyers; Allied aircrews then strafed the lifeboats to kill survivors. The Japanese 51st Division lost most of its staff, all its equipment and over three thousand soldiers.

To counter the growth in Allied air effectiveness, Admiral Yamamoto scraped together three hundred planes from the army and the carriers to attack Allied airfields throughout the Solomons and New Guinea. The raids inflicted insubstantial damage, but added to the severe attrition of the Japanese air forces. Meanwhile, the Americans were receiving more aircraft and pilots and introducing new and substantially improved models into the fighting. On the army air force side, the P-38 Lightning, with its great range and capacity to loiter at high altitude, was a serious threat to Japanese fighters. On the navy side, the introduction of the F6F Hellcat provided a margin of superiority to naval pilots in the air-to-air arena.

The result was similar to what was happening to the Luftwaffe at this time. Air battles over the Solomons and New Guinea depleted the few remaining experienced Japanese pilots; their replacements received less and less training and consequently died at an increased rate. Having done little to prepare a solid base, the Japanese proved profligate with the lives of their fliers and then desperately had to fill the seats left by the destruction of the highly skilled pilot force with ill-trained and ill-prepared pilots. Saburo Sakai, returning to training with one good eye, records:

> I found it hard to believe, when I saw the new trainees staggering along the runway, bumping their way into the air. The navy was frantic for pilots, and the school was expanded every month, with correspondingly lower entrance requirements . . . everything was urgent! We were told to rush the men through, to forget the fine points. One after the other, singly, in twos or threes, the training planes smashed into the ground, skidded wildly through the air . . . It was a hopeless task.

The Americans, on the other hand, made good their losses. Their new pilots were given increased flying time and now that they had superior aircraft they held a double advantage. Symptomatic of the situation was the ambush of Admiral Yamamoto's aircraft by P-38s in mid April 1943. Alerted by intelligence, the Americans pushed out a killing team of Lightnings, fitted with special drop tanks, to the furthest extent of their range. Off southern Bougainville, the Americans shot down the Japanese admiral's aircraft.

THE AMERICAN TIDE

Worse was coming for the Japanese. In the summer of 1943, the fruits of the great American shipbuilding programme, which had begun in 1938, showed up in the Pacific. By the autumn of 1943 five Essex class carriers had arrived at Pearl. These carriers held almost a hundred aircraft; they were faster and substantially more heavily armed with anti-aircraft guns than earlier US carriers; they were the opening wave in a tide of American industrial production. At the same time six Independence class carriers were also arriving; about half the size of the Essex class, they carried half the aircraft, but were equally fast and manoeuvrable. Altogether the US Pacific Fleet was to receive a new fast carrier almost every month. These carriers also carried the new aircraft types that had already reversed the technological balance in the Pacific in favour of the Americans. By the end of 1943 the US Navy had ten heavy carriers to four for the Japanese, nine light carriers to five, and thirty-five escort carriers to three. By the autumn of 1944 Third/Fifth Fleet was bigger than all the rest of the navies in the world combined.

The swelling size of both the carrier fleet and the aircraft available allowed the US Navy to execute an unprecedented campaign. Liberally supported with supply and repair ships, and floating dry docks, as well as oilers, the Pacific Fleet could remain at sea indefinitely. In 1944 its command would change back and forth between two fleet commands – the Fifth Fleet under Admiral Raymond Spruance and the Third Fleet under Halsey – as one conducted an operation while the other planned the next move. The swelling US fleet led to considerable squabbling between army and navy over control of forthcoming operations. MacArthur mobilized political support in the United States for the position of supreme command in the Pacific. The navy, however, had no intention of placing itself under MacArthur's control. The result was a bifurcated command structure which divided the American effort between MacArthur's drive from New Guinea towards the Philippines and Nimitz's drive across the central Pacific. Both bypassed Japanese garrisons on islands throughout the Pacific and took advantage of

Allied air superiority to leap-frog across the island chains which the Japanese had thought would provide security. Nevertheless, by dividing their strength, the Americans exposed themselves to a Japanese riposte; only the intelligence advantage that Magic conferred and the incapacity of the Japanese to concentrate their forces prevented the Americans from suffering a serious setback.

The central Pacific drive began in November 1943, with the marine assault on Tarawa Atoll in the Gilberts. American carrier aircraft isolated the Japanese garrison from support by Japanese land-based air power. Then the marines stormed ashore; a series of costly miscalculations by the marines increased the effectiveness of the Japanese land-based defences. But in the end the marines got the island, and American land-based air power now dominated the Gilberts. The next step was an inspired move by Nimitz. The American admiral ordered a strike at Kwajalein, at the centre of the Marshall chain. He ran into opposition from nearly all his subordinates, including Spruance, who argued that Japanese air bases near Kwajalein would place the amphibious landing in danger and expose the fleet to unacceptable risks from Japanese air attacks. They argued the next attack should target one of the eastern Marshalls, where US land-based air power in the Gilberts could support the invasion.

But Nimitz persisted; the US Navy would now find out whether its carriers could operate independently of supporting land-based aircraft. The Americans first hammered the Japanese bases in the Marshalls with long-range, land-based attacks from Makin and Tarawa. Then, in January 1944, the carriers rolled in to finish the job; within two days there were hardly any Japanese aircraft left on the chain. Although the Japanese had a large force on Kwajalein, they had not had the time to dig formidable defences, so swift was the American descent. Moreover, the US Navy embarked on a more intense and effective air and sea bombardment of Japanese positions than at Tarawa. The results of American superiority were twofold. In mid February Kwajalein fell, more quickly than expected, and the Americans then grabbed Eniwetok

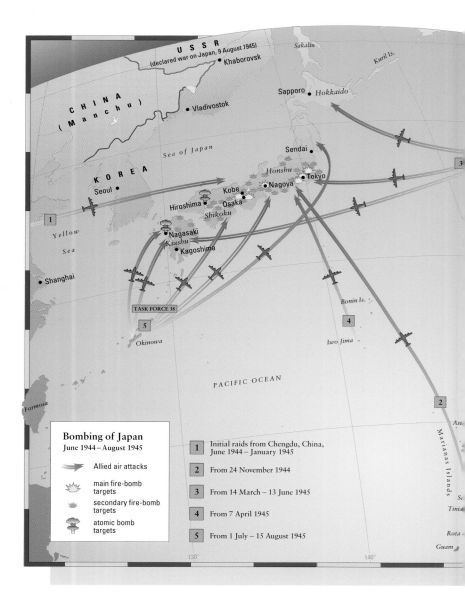

USSR
(declared war on Japan, 9 August 1945)
Khaborovsk

Sakalin

Kuril Is.

CHINA
(Manchu)

Vladivostok

Sapporo • Hokkaido

Sea of Japan

Sendai

KOREA

Honshu

Seoul •

Kobe
Hiroshima •   Nagoya • Tokyo
Osaka •

Shikoku

Yellow
Sea

Nagasaki
Kiushu
• Kagoshima

Shanghai

Bonin Is.

TASK FORCE 38

Okinowa

Iwo Jima

PACIFIC OCEAN

Formosa

Bombing of Japan
June 1944 – August 1945

Allied air attacks

main fire-bomb
targets

secondary fire-bomb
targets

atomic bomb
targets

1   Initial raids from Chengdu, China,
    June 1944 – January 1945

2   From 24 November 1944

3   From 14 March – 13 June 1945

4   From 7 April 1945

5   From 1 July – 15 August 1945

Marianas Islands

Sa
Tinia

Rota

Guam

130°   140°

and its surrounding atolls at the end of the Marshalls. In three months, Nimitz's forces, drawing on naval-borne aircraft, had projected US power 1,300 miles through the Japanese island defences that were supposed to provide a glacis to protect Japan. The Americans now had an ideal jumping-off position for attacking the Marianas, from which they could launch long-range bomber raids on the home islands.

AIR WAR IN THE CHINA–BURMA–INDIA THEATRE

The collapse of the British colonial position in South-east Asia had allowed the Japanese to grab Burma as well as Malaya at minimum cost, and this threatened the British position in India. However, the Japanese, still burdened by the ground war in China, had neither available reserves nor a logistic system capable of invading India. But the British could not know that and so they aimed to throw the Japanese back from the Burmese–Indian frontier. The Americans also exhibited interest in the theatre – not to protect India, but because of the rather bizarrely optimistic notions they held about the potential of Chiang Kai-shek's China. Thus, there was co-operation between the Anglo-American allies in the theatre, but they had different objectives. In the case of the British, air power proved of considerable utility in the war against the Japanese, but the basic problem was that it took two years for the finest British general of the war, Lt. Gen. William Slim, to square away a

THE SETTING SUN

On 15 June 1944 the first US bombers to attack the Japanese mainland since the Doolittle Raid three years earlier, were B-29 Superforts of the XXI Bomber Command based in Chengdu, China. It was the capture of the Mariana Islands that made large-scale B-29 raids a reality in 1945. Incendiary bombing of Tokyo and other major cities by up to 600 B-29s caused enormous damage and killed over 100,000 Japanese.

ragtag collection of British and Commonwealth troops into an effective fighting force. A dense canopy of jungle growth made it difficult for aircraft to attack enemy supply lines in Burma. Only when the Japanese attacked Imphal in 1943 could air power intervene to much effect. In late 1942 the British had formed a special commando force under the wildly eccentric brigadier, Orde Wingate, whose idea was to use small commando columns, supplied by air, to attack Japanese supply lines throughout northern Burma. The effort caused some disruption among the Japanese, and the aerial resupply worked quite well, but the force suffered heavy losses from combat and the ravages of disease. Most British military leaders did not judge these raids a success.

However, stung by Wingate's attacks, the Japanese invaded eastern India. With Allied air superiority and considerable support from transport aircraft, Slim shifted an entire division by air – troops, artillery and mules – in eleven days. Close air support from RAF fighter bombers proved useful in overcoming Japanese attacks. But the largest advantage was that Slim could supply his forces from the air, while British air attacks strangled the Japanese supply lines. In the end the Japanese offensive collapsed against overwhelming British air superiority. The weary, half-starved survivors of the Japanese Fifteenth Army then fell back into Burma.

The Americans had viewed the fighting in northern Burma only as a basis for getting supplies from India through to the Chinese. They believed it essential to reopen the Burma Road to supplement the airlift they were mounting over the Himalayas. But while the Americans possessed different strategic aims from those of the British, they were hardly in agreement among themselves or with their Chinese allies. At the start, a number of American leaders held too optimistic a view of Chinese capabilities – so much so that one of the premier US army officers of the interwar period, 'Vinegar Joe' Stilwell, was sent out to act as a military adviser to the Chinese Nationalists. Their leader, Chiang Kai-shek, however, had no intention of using his army, built up with

American aid, against the Japanese; rather he intended to use it to settle accounts with Mao Tse-tung's Communists when the war was over.

In addition to Stilwell, the Americans were represented by Major-General Clare Chennault, who believed that the war against Japan could be won by long-range bombers flying from Chinese bases. After a long drawn-out contest among Chiang, Chennault and Stilwell, the Chinese persuaded Roosevelt to replace Stilwell and follow Chennault's air-power strategy. By the summer of 1943 the Americans had established a great air bridge across the Himalayas to China, using mainly C-46 cargo aircraft. In August 1943 total tonnage reached 5,000 tons; by January 1944 Air Transport Command delivered 15,000 tons. But the effort was costly – the Americans lost an aircraft for every mile over the 'hump', a distance of well over 500 miles.

In the end, it was for nought. The build-up of fuel and ammunition allowed the Americans to deploy the first operational bombardment wing of B-29 'Superfortresses' to China. But the Japanese had not been sleeping. Even before the start of long-range US bombing operations, they had picked up what was afoot. Consequently, a major Japanese offensive aimed at eliminating the US air bases in China began in January 1944. Over the next ten months the Japanese chewed through the ineffective resistance offered by Chiang's troops, who had received little in the way of supplies from the delivery effort over the 'hump'.

US air power proved incapable of intervening in the ground battle in an effective manner, and Chennault had to watch as the Japanese drove his fighters and bombers from one base to another. In summer 1944 Headquarters, US Army Air Force, concluded that bases in the Marianas, in the process of being captured by Nimitz's drive across the central Pacific, offered a safer and more effective haven for the B-29 offensive against Japan. From that point, American interest in supporting Chiang, who had proved himself thoroughly corrupt and incompetent, waned. The China theatre became a backwater as the Japanese withdrew troops and resources, while the Nationalists and the Communists prepared for the coming struggle to control China.

THE JAPANESE DEFEAT

Throughout 1943 the Japanese fleet avoided a confrontation with US naval forces in the Pacific. The fall of Kwajalein and Eniwetok in early 1944, however, along with the neutralization of Japanese bases in the Gilberts and Marshalls, indicated to Japanese military leaders that the Americans would soon strike the Marianas. They were right; despite continuing squabbles fuelled by MacArthur's efforts to gain control of the entire theatre, Admiral Ernest King, commander-in-chief of the US Fleet, determined that the Marianas would be the next objective. There were some doubts from his subordinates in the Pacific. But King received enthusiastic support from Hap Arnold, who wanted the islands as bases for his costly B-29s. The Fifth Fleet, under Spruance's command, was now divided into Task Force 58, with fifteen fast carriers (nearly 900 aircraft), and Fifth Amphibious Force, with over 400 warships and amphibious ships and large landing craft. The targets were the islands of Guam, which the Japanese had seized early in the war, and Saipan.

The Japanese understood the importance of these islands, as well as the aerial threat their possession would pose to the home islands. The main Japanese fleet concentrated in the Tawitawi fleet anchorage between Mindanao and Borneo with nine carriers and over 500 aircraft; moreover, the Japanese prepared approximately 1,000 land-based aircraft to support their defensive efforts. They aimed to use the land-based aircraft to inflict heavy damage on the Americans, with the carrier aircraft and the battle line administering the *coup de grâce*. Japanese aircraft possessed one important advantage: range. But US aircraft were now superior in virtually every combat indicator, while American pilots enjoyed superiority over their Japanese counterparts – with the exception of the few Japanese survivors from the pre-war forces. The American plan was equally straightforward: Task Force 58 would first destroy Japanese land-based air power in the Marianas; then, it would prepare the way for the assaults, while awaiting the appearance of the main Japanese fleet, which Magic intercepts indicated would come out and contest the landings.

The Boeing B-29 Superfortress was the first USAAF strategic bomber which had twice the range while carrying twice the bombload of the B-17. Operating from bases on captured Pacific Islands from the beginning of 1945, the Superfortress became one of the principle Allied weapons in the war against Japan.

Thus began the battle of the Philippine Sea and the 'Marianas Turkey Shoot'. On 11 June US aircraft carried out extensive attacks throughout the Marianas. Over the next eight days the Americans reduced Japanese land-based air strength by 50 per cent at little cost to themselves. While marines were assaulting Saipan, the Japanese fleet moved from its bases. On 19 June the Japanese came within range of the Third Fleet and launched. Over the course of the day the Japanese flew 328 sorties and lost 243 carrier aircraft – an astonishing loss rate of 74 per cent. In addition they lost another fifty land-based aircraft.

On the evening of the 19th Spruance turned his carriers east to protect the landing forces – obviously to prevent another Savo Island. Early the next morning he turned west to pursue the Japanese. But not until late that day did the Americans discover the main Japanese fleet of six battleships and six carriers, with only thirty-five fighter planes remaining to protect them. Spruance ordered his aircraft to take off even though it was late and the Japanese were at the limit of US aircraft range. The American strikes did some damage to the Japanese and sank one carrier. But many of the returning aircraft ran out of fuel in the night. Only the fact that Spruance ordered the carriers to turn on their lights prevented really serious losses. The destruction of Japanese air power, naval as well as land-based, however, allowed completion of the conquest of Saipan and further landings on Guam and Tinian. The Americans now had bases from which they could mount an aerial offensive on the Japanese home islands. Engineering work immediately proceeded at full speed, while the logistical movement of aircraft supplies, bombs and fuel across the Pacific began.

With the capture of bases in the Marianas, American carriers ravaged the western Pacific and took out over one third of the 1,500 ground-based aircraft that the Japanese were gathering to defend the Philippines. So complete was US naval air superiority that Halsey urged Nimitz and MacArthur to forgo an invasion of Mindanao and land at Leyte in the middle of the Philippine islands. The Joint Chiefs approved the change and set the landing date for mid October. Not surprisingly, the Japanese guessed the next target would be the Philippines; they chose to commit their remaining fleet to the defence of the islands. While most of the Japanese carriers had escaped destruction in the battle of the Philippine Sea, they had lost their naval aircraft and pilots. Thus, the Japanese naval staff decided to use the carrier force as bait. Sailing from the home islands, they were to draw Task Force 58 away from the landing areas. There the Japanese main fleet, consisting of battleships and cruisers and based at Linga Roads near Borneo's fuel supplies, would strike the landing forces after moving through the various straits in the Philippine Islands.

The battle of Leyte Gulf was a confused and messy affair that came close to being a disaster for the Americans. But air power again played the crucial role in turning things to their advantage. The main Japanese battle force moved through San Bernadino Straits over the night of 23–24 October. Warned by Magic intercepts and reconnaissance aircraft, Halsey's aircraft blasted the Japanese and sank the super battleship *Musashi,* one of the three largest warships in the world. The great ship took nineteen torpedo hits and seventeen bomb hits before it finally sank. US carrier pilots, however, wildly overestimated the damage they had done to the attacking force. They also reported that the Japanese had turned back. They were correct in this last report, for a discouraged Vice Admiral Takeo Kurita, commander of the San Bernadino task force, had ordered a retreat. But on being informed of that move, Kurita's superiors immediately ordered him to reverse course and rethread the San Bernadino Straits.

As reports came in of the damage done to Japanese fleet units, Halsey received the news of the approach of enemy carriers from the north. He immediately turned all of Third Fleet northward, including not only the fast carriers, but the fast battleships as well. His forces would sink all four of the Japanese carriers. But the San Bernadino Straits were open to Kurita's force of four battleships and eight cruisers, which had a clear run to the American invasion fleet. That invasion fleet of attack transports and supply ships had only a light screen of naval support, six escort carriers and seven destroyers and destroyer escorts. In the early morning hours of 25 October, American lookouts, to their horror, spotted the pagoda-like structures of the Japanese heavy units bearing down on them. Nevertheless, despite overwhelming enemy superiority, American aircraft from the escort carriers, none of which possessed torpedoes or armour piercing bombs, fended Kurita's ships off until the Japanese admiral lost heart and fled back through the San Bernadino Straits. The Americans were lucky indeed to lose only one escort carrier. On the other side, the loss of four carriers, three battleships and ten cruisers in the various fleet battles represented the end of the Imperial Japanese fleet as a serious military force.

As the US Navy moved its carriers away from the Philippines, MacArthur's forces struggled to take Leyte against heavy Japanese reinforcements on the ground and in the air. American plans rested on the rapid capture and construction of airfields on Leyte, but Japanese resistance proved stronger than anticipated, while constant rains proved a nightmare for those constructing airfields. Moreover, while the quality of Japanese pilots was continuing to decrease, the introduction of the kamikazes, with pilots willing to crash their aircraft into US ships, added a vicious wrinkle to what was already a nasty war. American air defences destroyed the majority of inbound kamikaze planes, but some slipped through; over the next ten months the Japanese sank or damaged forty-six cargo ships.

While the clearing of the Philippines went ahead, the great build-up of US strategic bombing forces continued in the Marianas. The B-29, which executed the strategic bombing campaign against Japan, was the outcome of one of the most costly developmental programmes embarked on in 1940. With a range of over 4,000 miles when fully loaded, the B-29 had represented a quantum leap in aircraft technology. By the end of 1942 the developmental process had already cost $3 billion. The first proto-types and production models ran into a host of problems; most seriously, engines had a distressing habit of catching fire when under heavy loads. By 1943 some USAAF officers were calling the aeroplane 'the Annihilator' – and not for its capacity to harm the enemy.

American persistence paid off. By the late autumn of 1944 the Americans were ready to restart the strategic bombing of the Japanese home islands from the Marianas. To head this offensive, Arnold chose Brigadier Haywood Hansell, who had been one of the foremost theorists on precision bombing in the 1930s. But as in Europe, the Americans ran into problems that made strategic bombing more difficult in practice than air-power theory had predicted on the basis of results in Arizona. First, weather over Japan proved no more co-operative than it had done over Europe. Clouds often obscured targets, while high winds at altitude made accurate bombing almost impossible. Moreover, precision targets on the ground were difficult to identify, since Japanese industry was decentralized, while the radar station on Iwo Jima provided the Japanese with advanced warning. Finally, XXI Bomber Command ran into all the maintenance and supply problems inherent in introducing a new aircraft to combat with bases in the forward area.

In January 1945 Arnold relieved Hansell and replaced him with Major-General Curtis LeMay, a hero of the Schweinfurt/Regensburg raid. LeMay, a cigar-smoking, ferocious graduate of Ohio State University, quickly fixed the supply and maintenance problems with typical toughness. But his command's bomber losses were beginning to reach unacceptable levels. The costly marine assault on Iwo Jima in

February 1945 substantially reduced the warning time the Japanese had of American air raids and as a result reduced the losses. In addition, Iwo Jima served as a recovery base for damaged B-29s that could not make it back to their bases, and enabled P-51s to escort the bombers to the home islands. But bombing accuracy continued to plague the Americans. In February 1945 LeMay began to experiment with dropping incendiaries on Japanese cities. The results were encouraging enough for him to alter XXI Bomber Command's tactics. Unimpressed with the effectiveness of enemy flak and plagued by bad weather, LeMay followed the path blazed by Bomber Command against Germany; the Americans now began bombing at lower altitudes. With over three hundred B-29s at his disposal, LeMay then had the armour and most guns stripped from some bombers to attack Japan's cities in a night bombing offensive aimed at shocking the Japanese into surrendering. With its cities largely constructed of wood and paper, Japan was highly vulnerable to such an attack.

The new tactics worked to perfection in the first raid: the great fire-bombing of Tokyo. The attack caught the Japanese by surprise: they possessed virtually no night-fighter defences; their anti-aircraft defences were minimal; and, worst of all, the fire-fighting capabilities of Tokyo were completely inadequate. Over the night of 8/9 March the B-29s dropped their incendiaries from low altitude and created a firestorm that enveloped the Japanese capital. By the morning an area of sixteen square miles had been burned; 83,000 were dead and a further 41,000 injured, a far more terrible result than either Hamburg or Dresden. LeMay then turned his command on the major Japanese cities. It devastated Nagoya, Osaka, Yokohama, Kawasaki and Kobe, along with a large number of provincial towns. As naval historian Ronald Spector notes in *Eagle Against the Sun*:

> And yet, some bomber crews flying through the dense clouds
> of smoke and ash, smelling the smell of burning cities, whose
> flames were visible to aviators from a distance of over fifty

miles, probably realized that this was something new, something more terrible than even the normal awfulness of war. Machines of war had achieved the power to match natural catastrophes in destructiveness and, as in natural disasters, neither the young nor the very old, the innocent or the helpless, were spared.

But it was not just Japan's cities the B-29s savaged. In March LeMay's B-29s began an extensive mining campaign against Japan's inland seas and so shut down civilian and economic maritime traffic. By the spring Japan's position was hopeless.

Diplomatic historians have often used a series of messages from the Japanese Foreign Office to its Moscow embassy asking Stalin to intervene as evidence that the Japanese were ready to quit and that this fact was known to American civilian and military leaders. What such academic exercises ignore are two factors: first, that the military was still firmly in control of Japan and, second, that what the US leaders were reading were decrypts of *military* messages traffic and these indicated that Japan's military leaders had no intention of surrendering and remained indifferent to the sufferings of Japan's civilian population.

Moreover, the military decrypts underlined the fact that a massive build-up was occurring on Kyushu over the late spring and into summer 1945 – a build-up that increased the island's garrison from approximately one hundred thousand to a level of nearly five hundred thousand soldiers. What made those numbers particularly frightening to American leaders were the casualties that US forces had suffered on Iwo Jima (nearly seven thousand dead and twenty thousand wounded) and on Okinawa. In the latter case fierce fighting had begun with American landings in April 1945 and lasted throughout May. The Americans had attacked Okinawa to serve as the main base for the forthcoming invasion of Japan and they ran into an exceptionally well-conducted defence by the Japanese Thirty-second Army of over seventy thousand troops. Okinawa turned into one of the bloodiest battles of

The most famous Superfortress was B-29-45-MO named Enola Gay *belonging to the 393rd Bombardment Wing of the 509th Composite Group. Based at Tinian in the Marianas,* Enola Gay, *piloted by Colonel Paul W. Tibbets, dropped the first atomic bomb on Hiroshima on 6 August 1945.*

the Pacific war and suggested what the Americans and their allies could expect in an invasion of Japan.

Because of the extended nature of the fighting and the size of the effort, the US fleet remained in an exposed position around the island. There it came under a series of massive assaults from Japanese kamikaze planes launched from the home islands and from Taiwan. On 7 April no less than seven hundred Japanese aircraft, half of them kamikazes, struck the American fleet. Over a period of six weeks the Japanese subjected the US fleet to ten massed kamikaze attacks of between fifty and three hundred aircraft. The pilots were unskilled; the great majority were shot down by combat air patrols and anti-aircraft fire. Moreover, most who got through the aircraft screen either missed their targets or were blown out of the sky by massive anti-aircraft barrages put up by the ships.

But those that succeeded in getting through inflicted terrible damage on the ships that they hit, for not only did their bombs impact on their victims, but the fuel and aircraft travelling at maximum speed caused fires, explosions and considerable damage. Here the Royal Navy made a significant contribution with its fleet carriers, that had recently arrived in the theatre; they had been ungratefully received by Admiral King in Washington, but not by those in the theatre itself. British carriers possessed significantly fewer aircraft, but their flight

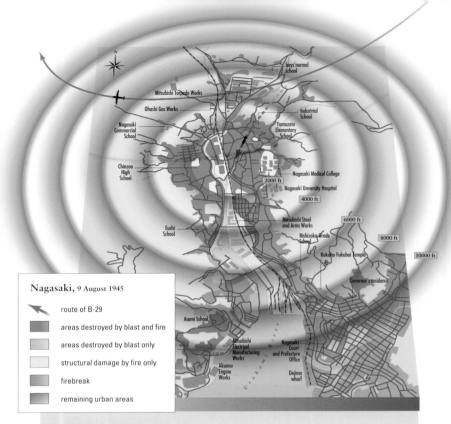

Labels on map:
boys' normal school
Mitsubishi Torpedo Works
Ohashi Gas Works
Industrial School
Nagasaki Commercial School
Yamazato Elementary School
Chinzoo High School
Nagasaki Medical College
2000 ft
Nagasaki Unversity Hospital
4000 ft
Euchi School
Mitsubishi Steel and Arms Works
6000 ft
Nishizoka-Brade School
8000 ft
Kokuho Fukubai Temple
10000 ft
Governor's residence
Asami School
Mitsubishi Electrical Manufacturing Works
Nagasaki Court and Prefecture Office
Akunou Engine Works
Dejima wharf
Urakami River

END GAME

The damage caused to the Japanese coastal city of Nagasaki, Kyushu by the second atomic bomb, a plutonium device nicknamed 'Fat Man' producing a yield of 18 kt, to be dropped on Japan, stretched almost half a mile from the epicentre of the explosion, killing more than 35,000 people.

decks were heavily armoured and could therefore absorb kamikaze hits better than their American counterparts. The land campaign on Okinawa inflicted over 60,000 casualties on the American marines and soldiers, while the attacks on the American fleet killed over 5,000 sailors and wounded another 5,000. The combined casualties equaled the number of Japanese soldiers killed on Okinawa – a grim hint to American political and military leaders of what might be in store in the coming invasion of Kyushu, Operation Olympic, scheduled to

The second atomic bomb, nicknamed 'Fat Man', dropped on Japan from B-29 Bock's Car *piloted by Major Charles W. Sweeney, exploding over Nagasaki on 9 August 1945 as part of Project* Alberta. *Six days later Japan surrendered unconditionally.*

take place on 1 November 1945. It was to be followed, if necessary, with Operation Coronet, landings on Honshu in the spring of 1946.

But that invasion never happened. It was forestalled by the great research project the United States had embarked on in the early 1940s, the Manhattan Project – the construction of the world's first atomic weapon. From the perspective of those who would be involved in the coming invasion (no-one in the Pacific doubted that it would come), the atomic bomb appeared a godsend. Paul Fussell's article in the 1980s, 'Thank God for the Atomic Bomb', underlines the attitude of those who would have been in the front lines – Fussell was an infantryman at the time.

In the early morning hours of 6 August 1945, three B-29s appeared in the air space over southern Japan. Japanese defences took little notice; not only was there no aviation gas for interception missions, but the three aircraft appeared to be too small to be part of a bombing force – perhaps they were another weather or reconnaissance mission. The lead aircraft, *Enola Gay*, piloted by Colonel Paul Tibbets, was in fact carrying the first atomic bomb. At 08.15 Tibbets' bombardier dropped the bomb and forty-five seconds later much of the city of Hiroshima disappeared in a flash. Nearly 100,000 people died almost immediately; tens of thousands died later from radiation poisoning. Yet initially Japanese military leaders took relatively little notice of the bomb. The Soviet invasion of Manchuria followed immediately on the heels of Hiroshima. Two days later the Americans dropped a second atomic bomb on Nagasaki; this time 35,000 died. The attack on a second city suggested that the Americans had more such weapons. Still the Japanese military leadership was divided as to whether to continue the war. But with his advisors unable to express a clear decision, the emperor, with great personal courage, stepped in and announced that his government would accept the Potsdam Declaration. The war in the Pacific was over.

Conclusion

Air power, as it had in the European war, proved of critical importance in the American victory. But in contradiction to the claims of pre-war prophets, air power had not by itself proved decisive (with the possible exception of the atomic bombs). Instead it had been an 'enabler' that had played to the organizational and industrial strengths of the United States. The Japanese had begun the war with a considerable advantage, underlined by their victories in the first six months of the war. But then the laws of attrition assumed control, and the Americans over the next year entirely wore away the Japanese advantages.

At that point, in the last half of 1943, the great flood of US industrial production, backed up by a great training and logistical establishment, took over. The arrival of the Essex and Independence class carriers with a new generation of fighter and torpedo-bomber aircraft, as well as land-based aircraft in vast numbers, swamped the Japanese defences. The drive across the central Pacific resulted in the capture of bases in the Marianas that made the destruction of Japan's cities by long-range bombing possible. Yet, despite the destruction of their cities, the destruction of their navy, the collapse of their shipping and the capture of major islands directly off the home islands, the Japanese military still argued for resistance. Only the atomic bomb, weapons of absolute destruction, confirming the darkest predictions of air-power advocates, brought the militarists in Tokyo to surrender and thus prevented the slaughter of hundreds of thousands of soldiers on both sides, as well as millions of Japanese civilians. Perhaps the dropping of those weapons served another important purpose: it served as a grim warning for the superpowers during the period of the Cold War of the enormously destructive powers of nuclear weapons.

Biographies

D. C. BENNETT (1910–86) Air Marshal Donald Bennett, an Australian-born officer, was one of the most innovative of the senior RAF leaders in the Second World War. Initially, he was responsible for organizing the transport of US-manufactured aircraft across the North Atlantic. After surviving and escaping being shot down over Norway and escaping via neutral Sweden, in 1942 he became commander of the RAF's Pathfinder Force to guide strategic bombers over Germany. Bennett remained one of the strongest innovators in tactics and operations throughout the remainder of the war. He would prove one of the harshest critics of Harris's conduct of the battle of Berlin.

OSWALD BOELCKE (1891–1916) Boelcke was one of the first and possibly the greatest fighter pilot of the First World War, who emphasized the need for an advantageous position before beginning an attack. He was awarded the Pour le Mérite, the 'Blue Max' in January 1916 for shooting down his eighth aircraft, and was one of the first heroes of the air war. In September 1916 he worked to establish the German *Jagdstaffeln*, the fighter squadrons responsible for shooting enemy fighters out of the sky, clearing the way for German reconnaissance planes. He was a great teacher, and trained von Richthofen, who later said, 'Whatever Boelcke told us was taken as Gospel'. Boelcke was killed in a mid-air collision in October 1916, and mourned by his colleagues in a great funeral in Cambrai cathedral.

JAMES DOOLITTLE (1896–1993) Talented, aggressive and versatile, 'Jimmie' Doolittle began his military career in 1917, and in 1922 he completed the first flight across North America in less than 24 hours. He was a premier fighter pilot in the US Army Air Corps in the 1920s, who spent the interwar years developing aircraft instruments and developed the first American blind bombing system. Having left the Air Corps in 1930, he was recalled to active service in 1940 and became the only non-regular officer to command a major combat air force in the Second World War. He led the raid of carrier-launched B-25s on Tokyo in April 1942, the first raid to take the war to the Japanese home islands, and received the US Medal of Honor for his work. Later in 1942 Doolittle was given command of the US Twelfth Air Force to prepare for Operation Torch, and in 1944 became commander of the Eighth Air Force which carried out strategic bombing against Germany. He left active duty in 1945, served on numerous Presidential Commissions thereafter, and was awarded his fourth star by President Ronald Reagan in the 1980s.

GIULIO DOUHET (1869–1930) Head of the Italian Army Aviation Service from 1918, Douhet was one of the first air-power theorists of the interwar years. Even before 1918, he was arguing that bomber attacks aimed at enemy population centres could bring wars to a quick conclusion, and that any effort devoted to armies and navies was a complete waste of money. Like his American counterpart, Billy Mitchell, Douhet earned great unpopularity by advocating a strong air force, and was court martialled in 1916 when he publicly denigrated Italy's airworthiness. He was released after the battle of Caporetto. His writings on strategic bombing, notably *The Command of the Air* (1921) were influential during the interwar years.

SIR HUGH DOWDING (1882–1970) Dowding began his career with the Royal Flying Corps, commanding squadrons on the Western Front during the First World War. As the head of the RAF's research and development establishment in the early 1930s, Dowding oversaw the development of radar and the Hurricane and Spitfire fighter aircraft. He became commander of Fighter Command in 1937 and transformed British air defence into an organized, cohesive system. He developed the system of fighter control by utilizing radio and radar communications to provide instant information regarding enemy activity to be passed directly from ground to air. Dowding's single-minded application of new technology undoubtedly saved Britain during the Luftwaffe's offensives in the Battle of Britain. Having served on a mission for the Ministry of Aircraft Production, he retired in 1942.

IRA EAKER (1898–1987) Eaker commanded the US Eighth Air Force in England in 1942–3, where he supervised the build-up of American strategic air power. An advocate of strategic bombing, he led the first US bombing offensive on western Europe, raiding Rouen in August 1943. He attended the Casablanca conference and convinced the chiefs of staff to continue US daylight precision raids in tandem with night sorties by the RAF. At the end of 1943 he was promoted to command the Allied air forces in the Mediterranean. He too was awarded his fourth star in the 1980s by President Ronald Reagan.

ANTHONY FOKKER (1890–1939) The original 'Flying Dutchman' (the title of his autobiography) Fokker taught himself to fly and constructed his first plane in 1911. Two years later, he founded the Fokker aircraft factory at Schwerin in Germany, which produced over forty highly successful planes for Germany during the First World War. He also devised the synchronizing interrupter gear system that prevented a machine-gun firing when the propeller blade was directly in front of it. In 1922 Fokker emigrated to the USA where he ran the Fokker Aircraft Corporation.

RENÉ FONCK (1894–1953) The greatest French ace of the First World War, Fonck was credited with seventy-five 'kills'. Blessed with incredibly sharp vision, Fonck amazed his colleagues with his ability to shoot down the enemy at great distances.

ADOLF GALLAND (1912–96) Galland was one of the most successful Luftwaffe aces of the Second World War. He fought with II Gruppe of *Jagdgeschwader* 26 during the Battle of Britain and in 1941 became Commander of the Fighter Arm, tasked with the defence of Europe. He encouraged Messerschmitt to build the new jet-engined 262 to match the American's P-51 Mustang, and consistently took the side of the pilots in demanding better equipment. Given command of an elite jet fighter squadron in January 1945, he was shot down in April and captured by the British.

HERMAN GOERING (1893–1946) Goering was a leading German ace in the First World War, who shot down twenty-two planes. A member of the Richthofen Squadron, he succeeded Richthofen as its commander after the death of the 'Red Baron' in 1918. In the postwar period he was an early member of the Nazi party and on Hitler's accession to power, the first and only commander of the Luftwaffe. He oversaw the development of the Luftwaffe into the formidable fighting force that entered the Second World War, but tended to make extravagant claims for the air force which it was unable to match. In May–June 1940 the Luftwaffe failed to finish off the BEF at Dunkirk, despite Goering's protestations about its capabilities. Later in the year Goering made a major error of judgment by moving the Luftwaffe's attack from British airfields to London, losing the initiative and, ultimately, the battle. At the battle of Stalingrad in 1942, Goering promised to supply the beleaguered Sixth Army with 500 tons of supplies a day, a figure that his overstretched forces could not fulfil. As the hostilities wore on, he sank into drug-induced lethargy and failed to provide the leadership necessary for the harsh battles of 1942–4, leaving decisions to his subordinates, Milch and Jeschonnek.

ARTHUR HARRIS (1892–1984) 'Bomber' Harris became head of Bomber Command in February 1942. Harris was responsible for putting Britain's strategic bombing campaign on a clear track, and for the ferocity and effectiveness of that effort. He dedicated his force to bombing German cities one by one, with the dual aims of devastating German industry and destroying civilian morale. Harris's single-minded approach has been questioned in terms of its military effectiveness as well as its morality.

MAX IMMELMANN (1890–1916) Immelmann was one of the founding fathers of fighter tactics and earned the title 'the Eagle of Lille' for his superb skill. He invented the 'Immelmann turn', a half-loop followed by a half-roll, in 1915.

HANS JESCHONNEK (1899–1943) A flying ace in the First World War, and the top graduate of his class at the Kriegsakademie, Jeschonnek became the Luftwaffe's Chief of the Air Staff in 1939. A firm believer in the Führer's genius, Jeschonnek committed suicide the day after Allied attacks on the V-2 establishment at Peenemünde and Schweinfurt.

GEORGE C. KENNEY (1889–1977) Kenney was one of the most innovative airmen of the Second World War. He commanded the Fifth Air Force under MacArthur, and transformed the tactics of his pilots and aircrew, enabling them to inflict a devastating defeat on the Japanese in the battle of the Bismarck Sea.

ALBERT KESSELRING (1885–1960) Considered highly talented by some historians and much overrated by others, Kesselring transferred from the army to the embryonic Luftwaffe in 1933. An advocate of strategic bombing, he supported Hitler's decision to attack London in 1940, but the failure of two of his daylight raids led to the postponement of Operation Sealion. Known to his aircrews as 'Smiling Albert', he also exercised a largely negative influence on Germany's air strategy in the Mediterranean from 1942 to 1943.

CURTIS LEMAY (1906– 90) LeMay was one of the premier American bomber commanders of the Second World War. He led the raid on Schweinfurt/Regensburg in August 1943. Two years later he was commander of the entire strategic bombing campaign against the Japanese home islands, and was responsible for developing the tactics that resulted in the fire bombing of Tokyo.

WILLY MESSERSCHMITT (1898–1978) A talented and imaginative aircraft designer, Messerschmitt began his career as a designer of sophisticated gliders, but in 1923 established his own business at Bamberg producing powered aircraft. In 1933 the Luftwaffe commissioned a new fighter plane and Messerschmitt produced the Bf 109 in 1935, which became the most successful German fighter of the Second World War. His most innovative plane, however, was the Me 262, the first jet fighter which entered active service in July 1944 and was responsible for the demise of at least one hundred US bombers. After the war, Messerschmitt continued his work in the field of aviation, producing a range of satellites, missiles and aircraft.

WILLIAM 'BILLY' MITCHELL (1879–1936) Mitchell was a leading American airman of the First World War and commanded the air campaign against the St Mihiel salient. He became a ferocious postwar advocate of strategic bombing in the US, arguing (unlike most of his contemporaries) that the enemy's air force must be defeated before a strategic bombing campaign could begin.

WILLIAM MOFFETT (1869–1933) The first commander of the US Naval Bureau of Aeronautics, Moffet played a vital role in preserving the independence of naval air power and in developing aircraft for carrier use.

CHESTER NIMITZ (1885–1966) Nimitz assumed command of US naval forces in the Pacific in late December 1941. He utilized his carrier forces first to thwart the Japanese in the battles of the Coral Sea and Midway in spring 1942, and then to achieve dominance over the central and western Pacific.

MANFRED VON RICHTHOFEN (1892–1918) The leading fighter pilot on the Western Front during the First World War, Richthofen is credited with shooting down eighty enemy aircraft in his scarlet Fokker triplane (which was the origin of his nickname, the 'Red Baron'). His squadron, known as the

'Flying Circus' devastated Allied air forces in 1917 and early 1918. His death in spring 1918 was an occasion of national mourning in Germany.

IGOR SIKORSKI (**1889–1972**) Sikorski was a Russian aviation pioneer who designed the first four-engined bomber, the Ilya Mouromet, in 1917. After the Russian Revolution, he fled to the US where he became a leading aircraft designer and was responsible for the development of the helicopter.

CARL SPAATZ (**1891–1974**) Spaatz was commander of the US army air forces in Europe for most of the Second World War. Responsible for American air power in the Mediterranean until 1943, he moved to England with Eisenhower. A strong advocate of air power, Spaatz co-operated closely with ground and naval commanders in achieving Allied objectives. In May 1944, he persuaded Eisenhower to undertake the great air campaign against the Reich's oil industry.

ARTHUR TEDDER (**1890–1967**) Tedder was the leading British airman in the Mediterranean theatre in the first years of the war, achieving close co-operation between air, land and ground forces. He became Eisenhower's deputy for the invasion of Europe, where he was to provide a singular contribution to Overlord's success by developing the transportation plan which was to cripple the German economy in the last months of the war.

HUGH TRENCHARD (**1873–1956**) Trenchard was the commander of the Royal Flying Corps units on the Western Front for much of the First World War. After commanding the RAF's strategic bombing force in 1918, he became head of the RAF for most of the 1920s.

Further Reading

GENERAL

Benjamin Franklin Cooling, *Case Studies in the Development of Close Air Support* (Washington, DC, 1990)

Carl von Clausewitz, *On War*, ed. and trans. by Michael Howard and Peter Paret (Princeton, NJ, 1976)

Alfred Hurley and Robert Ehrhart, *Airpower and Warfare* (Washington, 1979)

James S. Corum and Richard R. Muller, *The Luftwaffe's Way of War, German Air Force Doctrine, 1911–1945* (Baltimore MD, 1998)

Thomas H. Greer, *et al.*, *The Development of Air Doctrine in the Army Air Arm, 1914–1945* (Montgomery, AL, 1955)

Tony Mason, *Air Power, A Centennial Appraisal* (London, 1994)

Allan R. Millett and Williamson Murray (eds), *Military Effectiveness* (3 vols.) (London, 1988)

R. J. Overy, *The Air War, 1939–1945* (London, 1980)

Michael S. Sherry, *The Rise of American Air Power, the Creation of Armageddon* (New Haven, 1987)

Anthony Verrier, *The Bomber Offensive* (London, 1968)

FIRST WORLD WAR

Ralph Barker, *The Royal Flying Corps in France: From Mons to the Somme* (London, 1994)

Ralph Barker, *The Royal Flying Corps in France: From Bloody April to Final Victory* (London, 1995)

Malcolm Cooper, *The Birth of Independent Air Power* (London, 1986)

Richard P. Hallion, *The Rise of the Fighter Aircraft, 1914–1918* (Annapolis, MD, 1984)

Peter H. Liddle, *The Airman's War 1914–1918* (Poole, 1987)

Lee Kennett, *The First Air War, 1914–1918* (New York, 1991)

John Morrow, Jr., *The Great War in the Air, Military Aviation from 1909 to 1921* (Washington, DC, 1993)

John Morrow, Jr., *Building German Air Power, 1909–1914* (Knoxville, TN, 1976)

John Morrow, Jr., *German Air Power in World War I* (Lincoln, NB, 1982)

Williamson Murray and Allan R. Millett (eds), *Military Innovation during the Interwar Period* (Cambridge, 1995)

John C. Slessor, *The Central Blue: Recollections and Reflections* (London, 1956)

INTERWAR PERIOD:

Peter Fritzsche, *Nation of Fliers, German Aviation and the Popular Imagination* (Cambridge, MA, 1992)

Alfred F. Hurley, *Billy Mitchell, Crusader for Air Power* (New York, 1964)

H. Montgomery Hyde, *British Air Policy between the Wars, 1918–1939* (London, 1976)

Maurer Maurer, *Aviation in the U.S. Army, 1919–1939* (Washington, DC, 1987)

Malcolm Smith, *British Air Strategy between the Wars* (Oxford, 1984)

Barry Watts, *The Foundations of U.S. Air Doctrine, The Problem of Friction in War* (Montgomery, AL, 1984)

THE SECOND WORLD WAR (EUROPE)

Air Ministry, *The Rise and Fall of the German Air Force, 1933–1945* (London, 1948)

Earl R. Becker, *Under the Bombs, The German Home Front, 1942–1945* (Lexington, KY, 1986)

D. C. T. Bennett, *Pathfinder* (London, 1958)

Horst Boog, *Die Deutsche Luftwaffenführung, 1933–1945* (Stuttgart, 1982)

Conrad Crane, *Bombs, Cities, and Civilians, American Airpower Strategy in World War II* (Lawrence, KS, 1993)

W. F. Craven and J. L. Cate, *The Army Air Forces in World War II* (7 vols.) (Washington, DC, 1983)

Winston Churchill, *The Second World War* (Boston, 1949)

Richard G. Davis, *Carl A. Spaatz and the Air War over Europe* (Washington, DC, 1993)

Noble Frankland, *Bomber Offensive, The Devastation of Europe* (New York, 1970)

Max Hastings, *Bomber Command* (London, 1979)

Joel S. A. Hayward, *Stopped at Stalingrad, the Luftwaffe and Hitler's Defeat in the East, 1942–1943* (Lawrence, KS, 1998)

MacGregor Knox, *Mussolini Unleashed, Politics and Strategy in Fascist Italy's Last War* (Cambridge, 1982)

Francis K. Mason, *Battle over Britain* (New York, 1969)

Martin Middlebrook, *The Schweinfurt-Regensburg Mission, American Raids on 17 August 1943* (New York, 1983)

Martin Middlebrook, *The Berlin Raids, R.A.F. Bomber Command, Winter 1943–44* (New York, 1977)

Martin Middlebrook, *The Battle of Hamburg, Allied Bomber Forces against a German City 1943* (London, 1988)

Richard Muller, *The German Air War in Europe* (Baltimore, MD, 1992)

Williamson Murray, *German Military Effectiveness* (Baltimore, MD, 1992)

Williamson Murray, *Luftwaffe* (Baltimore, MD, 1985)

Michael J. Neufeld, *The Rocket and the Reich, Peenemünde and the Coming of the Ballistic Missile Era* (New York, 1995)

John Terraine, *The Right of the Line, The Royal Air Force in the European War, 1939–1945* (London, 1985)

Sir Charles Webster and Noble Frankland, *The Strategic Air Offensive Against Germany* (4 vols.) (London, 1961)

THE SECOND WORLD WAR (PACIFIC)

Samuel Eliot Morison, *The Two Ocean War* (New York, 1962)

Samuel Eliot Morison, *History of United States Naval Operations in World War II* (Boston, 1947–1962)

Gordon W. Prange, *Miracle at Midway* (New York, 1982)

Clark G. Reynolds, *The Fast Carriers, The Forging of an Air Navy* (Annapolis, MD, 1992)

Saburo Sakai, *Samurai!* (New York, 1975)

Ronald Spector, *Eagle Against the Sun, The American War with Japan* (New York, 1985)

Index

Figures in *italic* refer captions

Picture credits

Every effort has been made to contact the copyright holders for images reproduced in this book. The publishers would welcome any errors or omissions being brought to their attention.